UNDER WESTERN SKIES

SPELLBINDERS
FEARON'S FINEST FICTION

UNDER WESTERN SKIES

Prescott Hill
Janice Greene
Leo P. Kelley

FEARON EDUCATION
500 Harbor Boulevard
Belmont, California

Simon & Schuster Supplementary Education Group

SPELLBINDERS™
FEARON'S FINEST FICTION

Chamber of Horrors
Changing Times
Cloak and Dagger
Combat Zone
Foul Play
Strange Encounters
Under Western Skies
Winners and Losers

Cover Illustrator: James Gleeson

Copyright ©1991 by Fearon Education,
500 Harbor Boulevard, Belmont, CA 94002.

ISBN 0-8224-2804-0
Library of Congress Catalog Card Number: 90-82215
Printed in the United States of America
1. 9 8 7 6 5 4 3 2 1

Contents

Welcome to Skull Canyon

Prescott Hill

1

Jack Dade sat tall in the saddle. He turned and looked back at the mountains far behind him. It had been a hard ride. It was still dark when he'd broken camp that morning. Now the sun was high in the sky.

Dade wiped the back of his hand across his mouth. He must have already eaten five pounds of dust today. He had started west two weeks ago. From the very day he left Jefferson City, he'd been eating dust.

He guessed he was about a two hours' ride from Red Rock. "It's time for a little break, old girl," he said, swinging down from his horse.

"Take a good drink, Blazer. There's no telling when we'll get the next one."

He didn't have to speak twice. Blazer dropped her head and began to drink from the stream.

Dade took off his hat. He held it in the stream. When it was filled, he lifted it above his head. He let the water fall over him.

It splashed over his head and down his neck. It was cold. And it was good.

"This is more like it, Blazer," he said. "This is just what the doctor ordered."

He put his hat into the stream a second time. But as he lifted it, it was knocked from his hands.

A half second later, he heard the bang. It came from across the stream, to the left. He saw a little circle of smoke. It floated above a large red rock.

He thought it sounded like a Sharps buffalo rifle. He jumped to his feet.

"Go, Blazer!" he shouted. He hit her side with his hand. She took off running.

With a quick move, he reached for his holster. The pistol seemed to jump into his hand. He started firing and running.

He didn't aim. He just shot toward the circle of smoke as he headed for cover.

He saw a big log. It lay on the bank

above his side of the stream. It must have washed up there in the spring. The summer sun had turned it white.

He jumped over it just in time. A bullet whispered right above his head. Then he heard the bark of the rifle. It was a close call. But he was safe—for now.

He lay on the ground, not moving. Then he took bullets from his pocket. As he slipped them into his Colt .44 six-shooter, he shook his head. This was some welcome.

He waited for a minute. Then he stuck his hat up above the log. Another bullet just missed it. It smashed into the log. Little bits of wood went flying. He listened hard to the sound of the rifle. He was sure now. It was a one-shot Sharps buffalo rifle.

He got to his feet fast.

The man with the rifle would be busy. It was time to move.

He left his hat by the log. The top of it just showed.

Then he ran across the stream. When he got to the other side, he ducked behind a pile of rocks. He was very near the big red rock. He watched it—and waited.

Soon, he saw the rifle stick out from behind it. There was another circle of smoke and another loud bang.

Back by the log, his hat went flying.

Now! He ran as fast as he could toward the red rock. When he got there, he circled it. He ended up behind the man with the rifle.

"Drop it!" he shouted. "Put your hands in the air!"

The man with the rifle looked up. Dade's pistol was pointed right at his head.

It was hard to tell how old he was. His hair was white as snow. Dade could see that he had spent his life outside. Cold winters and hot summers had weathered his face. Wind and sun had left their marks. He might be 50. He might be 80. Dade couldn't decide.

The man set the rifle down and shook his head. "You got the drop on me," he said. "but don't think I'm finished yet!"

"I don't think anything, old man," Dade said. "I just want to know why you were shooting at me."

The man's eyes flashed. "Because you work for Cleary."

"Cleary?" Dade said. "Who's that?"

The man looked surprised. "You don't work for Tom Cleary?"

"Never heard of him," Dade answered.

"Well I'll be!" the old man said. "What a mix-up!"

"Mix-up?" Dade said. He kept his gun pointed at the man. "You tried to kill me!"

"No! No!" the old man explained. "Not kill you. Just frighten you off. I thought you were one of Tom Cleary's men. I thought you were here to make more trouble."

Dade looked hard at the man's face. He couldn't say why, but for some reason he believed him.

"All right, old man," Dade said, "let's talk."

"Sure," the old man said. "But it would help if you put that away first."

"Okay," Dade said. He put his pistol in its holster. Then he reached out his hand. "My name is Jack Dade. People call me Dade."

The old man shook hands. "Howdy, Dade. My name is Sims—Clarence Sims. Most people call me 'Cactus'. You can call me anything you want. Just don't call me late for dinner."

"I won't, Cactus," Dade said with a smile. He wiped his hand across his mouth.

"Come to think of it," Cactus said, "It's already past lunchtime. Will you come to my ranch and let me feed you? Maybe I can make up for putting a bullet through your hat."

"Well," Dade said with a smile, "I'm hungry enough to eat a cow."

"That's not on the menu. But you're welcome to what I've got if you can stand my cooking."

Dade laughed. "I'll give it a try," he said. He put two fingers to his mouth and blew. Blazer heard the whistle. She came running, her head high.

"Just a minute," Cactus said. He led his horse out from behind a pile of rocks. "This here is Lazy Legs." He patted the neck of the little spotted horse. Then he climbed into the saddle. "Follow me," he said. The two men headed for Skull Canyon Ranch.

CHAPTER

2

When Dade finished his second bowl of soup, he smiled. "That's good," he said. "I don't think I'll need that cow."

Cactus laughed and picked up his bowl. He put it to his mouth and drank from it. "Good to the last drop."

He set the bowl back on the table and looked at Dade. "Tell me," he said, "What brings you to this part of the country?"

"Just passing through," Dade said. "I'm headed west. But I have to stop in Red Rock. There should be a letter waiting for me there."

"With money in it, right?"

"I hope so," Dade said. He moved his soup bowl away. "Now," he said, "why don't you tell me about Tom Cleary?"

"Cleary!" Cactus said in a loud voice. "That rattlesnake!" He banged his fist on the table. "He was once my best friend. But that was a long time ago. Now I don't even like to hear his name!"

"What happened?" Dade asked.

"Well," Cactus said, "it's like this. Tom Cleary and I grew up together. We were like brothers. We did everything together. Work. Play. Everything. Later on, we even owned a ranch together."

Cactus sat forward in his chair. He looked across the table into Dade's eyes. "Well, one day it all changed. A new schoolteacher came to Red Rock. Sarah Gray was her name. She was really pretty. Smart, too. Tom Cleary and I both took a liking to her."

A sad look came into his eyes. His voice grew softer. "To make a long story short, Tom Cleary won out. Sarah married him. I went my own way. I sold him my half of the ranch and started this one. That was about 25 years ago."

Cactus shook his head. "Last spring, Sarah suddenly took sick. They don't know what caused it. She died a week later. And then the trouble started."

"What kind of trouble?" Dade asked.

"First I found part of a fence torn down. Then someone shot one of my longhorns."

"Longhorns?" Dade said. "No one raises longhorns these days."

"You're right," Cactus said. "They all go for white-faced cows now."

"Of course they do," Dade said. "The white-faced cows put on fat better. You really can't make any money on longhorns."

"I don't need the money. I already have enough. But I keep about 30 Texas longhorns for the fun of it. They help me remember the old days. They're mean and wild. Like me."

Dade smiled. He had worked Texas longhorns himself.

Cactus went on. "When Cleary started killing my cows, that did it. I kept my gun ready."

"Why would Cleary want to kill your cows?" Dade asked.

Cactus looked cross. "To trouble me. While Sarah was alive, we kept the peace. After she died, he tried to buy my ranch. But I wouldn't sell it. And now he thinks he can drive me off. He seems to think there isn't enough room around here for both of us."

Cactus banged his first on the table again. "He may be right. But it won't be me who leaves!"

The old man's face had become red. "The real trouble started last week. When I was out riding, someone took a shot at me."

He looked hard at Dade. "That's why I tried to run you off. I thought you were one of them."

"It sounds bad," Dade said. "But are you sure that Cleary's to blame?"

Cactus got an angry look on his face. "What do you mean? Who do you *think* shot at me? Do you think I just made it all up?"

"Hold on there," Dade said. "I don't take well to being shouted at."

"Is that right?" Cactus said. He jumped to his feet. "Well, you had your lunch. Now you can just get out of my home! And off my land!"

Dade gave him a long look. He stood up. "Thanks for the food," he said. He turned and headed for the door.

As he rode off, he heard the old man's voice behind him. It was a loud shout. "And don't come back. Next time, it won't be your hat I'll shoot!"

"Let's go, Blazer," Dade said. "We don't need to take that kind of talk. Not even from an old goat."

3

It was late afternoon when Dade got to Red Rock. He looked for a stable. He found one on a side street. The sign said "Danny Flynn's Horse Care."

Dade liked the place. It looked clean. Danny Flynn was a giant of a man. Dade could see he had a way with horses.

"I'll be leaving Blazer for the night," Dade told Danny. He dug into his pocket. He found a coin and gave it to the big man. "Make sure she has feed and water."

Dade started out of the stable but stopped. Turning back to Danny, he said, "Is there a good hotel in town?"

"The Red Rock Hotel," Danny said. "It's supposed to be pretty good."

"If it's got a bed and bath, it's good enough for me."

"It's got that," Danny said. "It's at the end of Main Street. A big yellow place. You can't miss it. Are you staying long?"

"No, I'm just passing through," Dade said. "By the way, where's the post office?"

"Next to the hotel, in Peter Dawson's store. Pete's got just about anything you might need. He can pull your teeth, too."

Dade made a face. "No, thanks. Getting my mail will do." He headed for Dawson's.

It was dark in the store. Still, Dade could see all kinds of things for sale. There was everything from pots and pans to guns and bullets.

A fat man sat at a table. He was eating a big piece of pie. He looked up at Dade and nodded his head. Then he went back to his pie.

"Nice day," said a voice from behind.

"Howdy," Dade said turning. A thin bald man stood there. He wore a red bow tie over his white shirt. In his hand he held a broom. He was sweeping around the fat man's chair.

"Just cleaning up," the man said.

"Are you Mr. Dawson?" Dade asked.

"That's right," the bald man said. "Can I help you?"

"I was wondering if there might be any mail for me here."

"Could be. What's your name?"

"Oh, I'm sorry. My name is Dade. Jack Dade."

"Why, yes," Mr. Dawson said. "I think there *is* a letter for you. Just a minute."

He swept a pile of red dust into the street. Then he went to the back of the store. A blue hat hung from a nail on the wall. He put it on. He smiled at Dade. "U.S. Mail" was written on the front of it.

Mr. Dawson went over to a large desk. He took his time looking through a pile of mail. At last he took a letter from the pile. He held it up close to his eyes. Then he turned to Dade.

"What was that name again?"

"Jack Dade."

Mr. Dawson smiled. "John Dade?"

"That's right," Dade said. It was the letter he was looking for. The only person who called him "John" was his uncle.

When Mr. Dawson gave him the letter, Dade held it up to the light from the window. "Was there anything else?" he asked.

"No," Mr. Dawson said. "That's all."

Dade didn't look happy. "I was hoping for some money," he said.

He opened the letter. There was no check, just one sheet of note paper. It was bad news.

The letter said that business had not been good. His uncle was supposed to send him money. Now he might not be able to do so for another two weeks, if then. Dade put the letter away. He had only a few dollars left. There would be no bed and bath tonight.

"No money, I guess," Mr. Dawson said.

"No," Dade said. "Nothing."

Then a voice said, "Looking for work, cowboy?" It was the man who'd been eating the pie. But the pie was gone now.

"I guess I am," Dade said.

"Try the Double Diamond Ranch. I hear they need hands."

"Where's that?" Dade asked.

The fat man stood up. He was short. His feet were the smallest Dade had ever seen on a man. He walked over to the door. He pointed across the street to a barber shop. "The owner is getting his hair cut now. You can ask him."

"I'll do that," Dade said. He stuck out his hand. "Jack Dade's the name. I thank you for your help."

The fat man shook hands. "You're welcome," he said. "My name's Jason Harper. If you decide to stay around, come by and see me. I own the Red Rock National Bank. It's a good safe place to keep your money."

"I'll remember that," Dade said, "if I ever get any money."

Dawson came over with his broom. Harper had left a trail of red dust. "Look out," Dawson said. He swept the dust out the door.

Dade thanked Harper again. Then he headed out the door. As he did, he bumped into a man coming in.

"Watch where you're going," he said to Dade. "Who do you think you are?"

"Sorry," Dade said. "I didn't see you."

The man was about 20 and was dressed in well-worn cowboy clothes. He seemed to be enjoying his own anger. "I guess you didn't, you fool!"

"Hold it," Dade said. "I told you I was sorry. There's no need for name calling."

"Is that right?" the cowboy said. "Well, *I'll* call you anything I want." He pulled back his arm and threw a punch at Dade.

Dade had done a lot of fighting in his time. But he had never learned to like it. With a quick step to the side, he ducked the punch. His own punch hit the man on the jaw.

The man didn't say a word as he dropped to the ground.

Dade got a good look at him. He was more a boy than a man, really. Dade shook his head. The young ones always want to fight.

"That was some punch."

Dade turned to see who was talking. Then he began to laugh. Half the man's face was white with shaving soap.

The man laughed, too. "I was getting a shave," he said. "I saw the fight out the window."

The man on the ground rubbed his jaw. He looked up at Dade and the other man.

"Get up, boy," the other man said. "We've got work to do."

He looked at Dade. "Can you take care of cows as well as you can fight?"

"When I have to," Dade said.

"Well, I need another hand," the man said. "I own the Double Diamond Ranch."

"I could use a job," Dade said. He stuck out his hand. "My name is Jack Dade."

The man took Dade's hand. "Mine is Tom Cleary." He pointed to the man Dade had punched. "This here is my son Jed."

4

Dade stretched out on the bunk. He put his hands behind his head and closed his eyes.

He had been at the Double Diamond Ranch for a week now. But it had been several years since he last worked on a ranch. How many jobs had he held since then?

He had worked in a gold mine. He had driven a stagecoach. He had been a buffalo hunter for the army. He had even been a sheriff for a while in Texas.

And now he was back punching cows.

It would have to do for a while. When his money came, he would head west again. Maybe he'd go all the way to San Francisco. Perhaps he could start some kind of business there.

This train of thought was broken by a question from Jed Cleary.

"Say, Dade, can I ask you something?" Jed's bunk was next to Dade's.

Dade opened one eye. "Sure, Jed. What is it this time?"

Dade liked Jed. The kid was a hothead, but Dade knew that would change. After their short fight, the two had become friends.

Dade had about 15 years on Jed. The young man stuck close to him. He watched everything Dade did. He asked a lot of questions.

This time Jed asked, "Will you teach me how to fight?"

Dade laughed. "I can tell you a few things, I guess. First off, don't pick fights. You'll get to see enough trouble. You don't have to go looking for it."

Jed rubbed his jaw. It no longer hurt from Dade's punch. He shook his head. "I know that now. But I want to learn about boxing. About trick punches and such."

Dade laughed. "Let me rest a bit. Tonight I'll give you a boxing lesson."

"Will you really?" Jed's face lit up in a smile.

"Yes," Dade said. "Now no more questions for a while, okay?"

Dade closed his eyes again, smiling. He liked the whole Cleary family—Jed, his big brother Billy, and Tom Cleary, too.

The father was a man of few words. He drove his men hard. But he worked as hard as any of them.

Dade had asked Jed about his father and Cactus Sims. Jed didn't know much. And brother Billy didn't know very much, either. Their father and Sims stayed away from each other. And Tom Cleary had told his men to keep clear of Skull Canyon. That was about all the two boys knew.

Dade himself had seen the bad side of Cactus Sims. The man got angry too fast. Dade couldn't blame Tom Cleary for keeping clear of old Cactus.

Well, Dade thought, it wasn't his business. He had other things to worry about.

Just then, he heard the ringing of iron on iron.

"Time to eat," Jed said.

Dade took out his watch. "It's a little early for the lunch bell," he said.

The bell kept ringing.

Finally Dade stood up.

Jed got up, too. Together with the other seven ranch hands, they headed for the big house.

Tom Cleary was coming out of it. He looked mad. "Who rang that bell?" he shouted.

"I did," said a short, round man dressed all in brown. It was Jason Harper, the banker.

"What's this all about, Harper?"

"Trouble." Harper said. "Big trouble."

"What is it?" Cleary asked.

"It's your son Billy. Somebody shot him in the back."

"Oh, no," Cleary said. "Is he . . . ?"

"Your boy is alive," Harper said. "But he's in bad shape. They took him to Doc Jones. Doc doesn't know if he'll come out of it or not."

"Who shot my brother?" Jed asked.

"We don't know for sure," the little man said. "I was in Red Rock when the stagecoach brought him in. The driver said he found him near Skull Canyon. I watched him while the driver went for Doc Jones. That's when Billy came to for a second."

"Did he say anything?" Tom Cleary asked.

"He just said one word, Tom. He said it over and over again.

"Well, what was it?" Cleary shouted.

Harper looked him in the eye. *"Cactus,"* he said. "Billy just kept saying *cactus."*

The color went out of Tom Cleary's face. His mouth got a tight look. "Cactus Sims!" he said. He looked at his ranch hands. "Get your guns, boys! And get ready to ride."

Cleary started back into the big house. On the top step he turned. "Get my horse!" he shouted to Jed.

In a moment, Tom Cleary came back out of the house. He was wearing his six-gun. A fire seemed to burn in his eyes.

He climbed up into his saddle and spoke in a loud voice. "First, I'm going to town to see Billy," he said. "Then I'm riding for Skull Canyon." He looked at his men. They were already in their saddles. "Are you with me?"

By the sound of their shouting, it was clear that they were.

Striking his hat against his horse's side, Cleary cried out, "Let's ride!"

The Clearys were on the move.

The Double Diamond Ranch was almost an hour's ride from town. On the way in, Dade did some thinking.

Was it likely that Sims had ambushed Billy Cleary? Old Cactus was a hothead. But so were the Clearys. Dade knew something about how men acted. And he didn't think Cactus would shoot a man in the back.

Yet Harper had heard Billy say Cactus's name. It didn't make sense.

When they got to town, Doc Jones had some good news. Billy was sleeping. He had lost a lot of blood, but he would pull through.

While they waited for Billy to wake, Dade made up his mind. If Cactus Sims had shot Billy, he would have to be tried. But, Dade said to himself, that job belonged to the law. It did not belong to the Clearys.

Without saying anything to the others, Dade slipped out of the doctor's house.

A minute later he was in the saddle. "Let's go, Blazer," he said. He started out of town, riding hard for the Skull Canyon Ranch.

5

Dade slowed Blazer when they were near the ranch house. He had tied a white cloth to a stick. He waved it in the air as he rode. Old Cactus would know enough not to shoot at a white flag.

Or at least Dade hoped he would.

Ten yards from the ranch house, he stopped.

Cactus stepped out the door. Held tight in his hands was his Sharps buffalo rifle. "What do *you* want?" he asked.

"I think you'd better hide out for a while."

"What?" Sims asked. His face got red. He brought the rifle up.

"Take it easy," Dade said. "I'm here to help you."

"Say what you have to say," Sims said. "And then get out."

"Someone ambushed Billy Cleary. Tom Cleary thinks you did it."

"Why, that . . . !"

"Hold on and listen!" Dade said. "I don't think you did it. But Tom Cleary does. He and his men are on their way here. And they don't mean to do you any good."

"Why, that . . . !"

"Save it for later!" Dade said. "You don't have much time."

"No one drives Cactus Sims off his land. Not today, tomorrow, or any other day. I'm staying!"

Dade shook his head. "Well, I thought that's what you'd say, Cactus. And I guess I'm going to stay here and help you." He got down from Blazer.

"You mean we'll fight together?" Cactus asked.

"No," Dade said. "I mean we'll try to *stop* a fight together." He turned toward the mouth of Skull Canyon.

A cloud of dust floated high in the air.

Sims looked at it. Cleary and his men were riding hard.

"All right, Dade," he said. "You got a plan?"

"Sort of," Dade said. "They have nine men. We have two. Still, it might work."

"Well," Sims said, "let's hear it."

A short while later, Tom Cleary brought his horse to a stop. He held up his hand. The men riding with him also stopped.

Cleary looked toward the ranch house.

"Come on out, Sims! You can't hide from me!" he shouted.

Cactus poked the end of his rifle out the door.

"Get off my land, Tom Cleary," said Cactus. "And stay off!"

"Not until I do what I have to do."

"You and your eight men, you mean."

Cleary got off his horse. He took a step toward the house.

"Never mind them," he said. "It comes down to just you and me. Man against man."

Cactus started to step out of the house. Then he stopped. He would give Dade's plan one chance.

"What do you want, Cleary?" Cactus said.

"You know what I want," Cleary said. "You shot my boy in the back. Let's see what you can do when a man is looking at you."

It was almost too much for Cactus. The heck with Dade's plan. Tom Cleary had gone too far! Cactus started to make a move.

Dade moved first.

He stepped out of the barn. As he did, he threw the rope. It was a good throw. It caught Jed Cleary clean. Dade pulled hard, and Jed fell from his horse. Dade rushed toward him and dropped down by his side.

Cleary's men turned. One drew his pistol and fired at Dade. The shot hit Dade's hand just as he was putting his right arm around Jed's neck.

Before the man could fire again, Tom Cleary grabbed him.

"Don't shoot! You might hit Jed!"

Cactus stepped out the door. He waved his rifle at the men. "All of you, put your guns away!"

Dade now had Jed in a tight hold. He held his pistol in his left hand.

"Listen, and listen good!" Dade said to Tom Cleary. "Jed stays put until you and your men are out of here. We don't want to hurt him. But if you cause trouble, anything could happen."

Tom Cleary looked at Dade with hate in his eyes. "I guess you were tied in with Sims all along," he said.

"Think what you like, Mr. Cleary," Dade said. "Just ride out of here. When I know you're far away, I'll let Jed go."

"Never mind me, Pa," Jed said. "Do what you have to do."

Tom Cleary looked at Jed. The boy was brave. He was a good son.

Cleary looked at Cactus and then at Dade.

"Don't think that this is the end of it," he said.

Dade started to say something. Then he stopped. He kept his gun on Jed. When Tom Cleary was out of sight, he put it away.

Dade looked at his right hand. It hurt, but he could stand it.

Dade held up his right hand while Cactus checked the bandage. It struck Dade funny. About six hours ago he had used that same white cloth as a flag. He had used it then to stop Cactus from shooting him.

Maybe he should have used it to stop Cleary's man from shooting at him, too.

Dade laughed, even though his hand hurt.

"I don't know why you're laughing," Cactus said. "You won't be able to use that hand for a week. Still, it should be okay. You're lucky. The bullet didn't break anything."

Jed sat in a chair across the room. His hands were tied behind him. He said nothing.

Cactus turned to Jed and said, "Son, you must be mad as a bear. Can't say I blame you. But there's no need to go hungry. I'll get you some food.

Jed shook his hand.

"All right," Cactus said. "Have it your way."

He turned to Dade. "We don't have to keep him tied up, do we?"

"No, I guess not," Dade said.

Cactus took out his pocketknife and went over to Jed. He made two quick cuts. The rope dropped to the floor.

Jed still didn't say anything. But he nodded his head in thanks to Cactus.

The old man winked at him.

Dade pulled his chair up in front of the young man. "I want you to listen closely, Jed," he said. "Whether you believe it or not, Cactus didn't shoot Billy. But I think I know how you feel. Still, I had to do it. A lot of men could have been badly hurt."

Jed's mouth stayed closed.

Dade went on. "I want you to tell your father that Cactus is coming to town to see the sheriff. He'll be there the day after tomorrow. By then, people will be thinking clearly."

From deep in Skull Canyon came the scream of a mountain lion. When the sound died down, Dade said, "You can bunk here for the night. Ride out first thing in the morning."

Jed shook his head and stood up.

"It's a long ride in the dark, Jed. But it's up to you."

Dade handed him his gun. "I took the bullets, Jed. Be sure you tell your father what I said."

Jed headed for the door. Dade and Cactus followed him. Outside, the young man started toward his horse. Then he stopped. He turned back to Dade. "I thought you were a friend," he said. "Now I know better."

Jed's horse was tied in front of the house. He climbed into the saddle. As he rode off, he shook his fist at Dade.

Dade went back inside. Cactus stayed out for a while. He watched until Jed was out of sight. Then he slowly walked back into the house.

Dade was over by the stove. He took some soup from a big pot. "Are you hungry?" he asked Cactus.

"No," the old man said. "I'll eat later."

Cactus took a chair by the fire. For a long time he was quietly lost in thought.

Dade watched him. He wondered what was on his mind. He guessed it had to do with young Jed Cleary. Then it hit him. Jed was Tom Cleary's son. But he was also the son of Sarah Gray Cleary.

Tom Cleary hadn't been able to sleep at all. It was still dark when he heard the sound of the horse.

He ran out of the house. "Jed, is that you?" he shouted. "Are you all right?"

Jed got off his horse. "I'm fine, Pa, just fine. How's Billy?"

Tom Cleary smiled. "Billy's okay. They should be bringing him here today."

"Great!" Jed said.

"One thing, though," Tom Cleary said. "Billy doesn't remember what happened. He doesn't know who shot him."

"But I thought Mr. Harper said . . ."

"I know," Tom Cleary said. "But Billy can't remember saying anything about Cactus Sims. Don't forget, he was shot off his horse. Doc Jones said that when he fell he took a bad knock on his head."

"Then who *did* shoot him?"

"I *still* think Cactus Sims did it. But I can't say for sure."

Jed thought for a while. "You know something, Pa? It seemed to me that Cactus was acting all right."

"Maybe so," Tom Cleary said.

Jed then told him about Dade's plan.

"Why won't they see the sheriff today?" Cleary asked.

"Dade wants people to cool off," Jed said.

It made sense. But Tom Cleary wasn't happy. "It just might be a trick," he said. "I'll go along with it. But I'm not through with Cactus Sims. You can be sure of that."

And I'm not through with Dade, Jed thought. *You can be sure of that!*

Jed woke up to a shout from outside. "Here he comes!"

He jumped to his feet and rushed out. A cloud of dust was coming toward the Double Diamond Ranch. Tom Cleary stood in the yard. "It's Billy!" the father said with a big smile.

Soon, the two horses pulling the wagon stopped. Doc Jones was driving. Mr. Harper sat next to him. Billy lay down in the back.

Doc Jones smiled. "I brought you your boy."

Billy looked up at his father and brother. "Hello Pa . . . Jed." There was not much color in Billy's face. But there was a wide smile on it.

Jed and another ranch hand carried Billy inside. Doc Jones went with them.

"Wait," Harper said to Tom Cleary. "Could I have a word with you?"

"Why, sure."

Harper climbed down from the wagon.

He looked around before talking. His voice was soft. "Help is on the way," Harper said.

"What do you mean?" Tom Cleary asked.

"I sent for a man to go up against Dade."

"Dade?"

"Yes. I found out that Dade's a gunfighter. Sims, I think, is paying him. You have no chance against him."

"But . . ."

"You don't have to worry. I sent a telegram to Central City. Help is on the way."

"I still don't know what you mean."

"Does the name Simon Moon ring a bell?"

Cleary looked surprised. "The killer?"

"Call him that, if you like," Harper said. "But he always stays inside the law."

Cleary shook his head. "I won't pay money to a killer."

Harper smiled. He rubbed his hands together. "You don't have to. That's all taken care of."

Cleary started to say something. Harper held up his hand. "This Dade is bad for us all. His kind brings trouble."

"Yes, but what about Moon? What about *his* kind, Mr. Harper?"

"When his job is done, he'll go away." A smile showed on Harper's face. "Sometimes we just have to fight fire with fire."

"I don't like it," Cleary said. "My fight is with Cactus Sims."

"We can talk about that later," Harper smiled again. "Let's go in now and see your boy."

Cleary nodded and headed for the house.

CHAPTER

7

Dade woke up with a start. *What in the world is that noise!* he wondered. He sat up and looked around. Something *smelled* good. But something else sure *sounded* bad.

Over at the stove, Cactus was cooking bacon. He was also singing a cowboy song. He sang loudly and off key.

"Do I hear a coyote barking?" Dade asked.

Cactus turned around and laughed.

"Good morning," Dade said. He gave Cactus a funny look. "You're pretty bright and sunny today."

Dade pulled on his boots. Then he got up and walked across the room to sit down at the table.

Cactus cracked four eggs into the pan.

"Well," Cactus said, "I'm trying to make up for the way I've been acting. I guess I treated you pretty badly."

"Badly?" Dade said. "Why, no. Let's see. All you did was run me off your land. And try to shoot me a few times. I wouldn't say you acted badly. Not for a mad old goat like yourself."

"I guess I have to take that," Cactus said. "I had it coming to me."

"I won't kid you anymore," Dade said.

"That's fine with me," Cactus said. Then he added, "Dade, I've got to ask you something."

"Ask away," Dade said.

"How come you don't think I shot Billy Cleary?"

Dade's answer was to the point. "Because if you did, Billy would be dead now. You're a crack shot. And that rifle of yours could just about stop a train. The gun that shot Billy had nowhere near that power."

Cactus looked him in the eye. "You're pretty sharp," he said.

"And there's another reason you couldn't have done it," Dade said.

Cactus put his head to the side. "What might that be?"

Dade rubbed his hand across his jaw. "Because of how you felt about his mother, Sarah Gray. You would never hurt one of her sons."

Cactus spoke in a soft voice. "No, I wouldn't."

"Tomorrow, we have to make the sheriff believe that."

"Why wait?" Cactus asked. "Let's ride into town after breakfast. You explain it to the sheriff. Get this whole problem cleared up."

"It might not be so easy," Dade said. "Not until we find out who did shoot Billy."

"Well, how are we going to do that?"

Dade stood up and began to walk about the room. "We don't have much to go on," he said. "But let's start with Tom Cleary."

Cactus made a face.

"Never mind how you feel about him. When did you last talk with him?"

"You were there," Cactus answered.

"No," Dade said. "Before that."

"I thought I told you. I haven't said a word to Tom Cleary for close to 25 years."

"Wait a minute," Dade said. "I thought he tried to buy your ranch."

"He did. But he didn't come here himself. He sent someone else to do his dirty work. A little pig-faced banker."

"Jason Harper?" Dade asked.

"That's the one. Do you know him?"

"I've met him," Dade said. He thought back to yesterday. He remembered how Harper had stood in Cleary's yard ringing the bell. The first time they'd met had been in Dawson's store. Harper had aimed him toward the Double Diamond Ranch.

This was getting interesting. "So," Dade went on, "Tom Cleary has never been here. That is, as far as you know."

"Not for 25 years."

Dade rubbed his jaw again. "But *Harper* was here." He was talking more to himself than to Cactus.

"What has that got to do with anything?"

"I don't know," Dade said. He started toward the door. "You eat my eggs. And stay close to the house. I'll be gone for only a little while."

"Do you think Cleary will come back?"

"Not today, I don't. But this is far from over."

Blazer stepped carefully, slowly picking her way along the trail. It had been a long day. She was getting very tired. Dade could tell by the sound she made as she took in air.

"Come on, girl," he said. He reached down and rubbed her chest. "It's time for a break."

He headed Blazer away from the canyon wall. When they reached the stream, he brought her to a stop.

"Easy, old girl," he said. He climbed down from the saddle. There was grass along the bank of the stream. He let the reins fall to the ground.

"You just take a rest," he said. "Have some dinner and cool off."

Blazer dropped her head toward the stream and drank.

Dade drank, too. Then he went over to a rock and sat down. It felt good to rest. The afternoon sun was going down. But it was still plenty hot.

As he got his second wind, his mind raced. He was looking for something. But what? That morning he had thought he would find an answer. Now it all seemed silly. Had he wasted a whole day?

Oh, well, he thought. There's no sense crying over spilled milk. He smiled at the sight of a baby bird. It seemed to dance about near the canyon wall. Then, just behind it, he noted something strange. There was a dead bush there that seemed out of place.

He got up and walked over to it. Someone had carried the bush there from the bank of the stream. When he pulled at it, he saw why.

It was being used to hide the mouth of a cave.

Dade had to bend low to see in. It was dark. But that presented no problem.

He went back to the stream. From his saddlebags, he got matches and a candle.

A few minutes later, he was inside the cave. Once past the mouth, he could stand up.

It was cool inside. The walls of the cave were wet. Suddenly, as he took a step, his feet started to slide. The cave floor was covered with wet red clay.

He pressed against the wall to keep from falling. The candle dropped to the ground and went out.

He found it and lighted it again. And then he noticed the marks in the clay. Someone else had slipped there not long ago.

He held the candle close to the cave floor. The shoe print was small. It must have been left by a child. Or a woman. Or . . .

"Of course!" Dade said. He let out a shout of joy. "Well, I'll be a monkey's uncle!" he said. Then he almost slipped again but caught himself just in time.

The pieces were fitting together.

By the light of the candle he inspected the cave. It went back almost 20 feet. Here and there, a bright spark seemed to shine from the wall.

Dade set the candle on the cave floor. Then he took out his pocketknife. He opened it and pushed the end of it into a crack in the wall. He dug around for a while. Finally, he pulled out something thin and flat. He looked at it in the light from the candle.

He smiled. Then he folded the knife and put it away. He put the tiny piece he had cut out into his shirt pocket.

He didn't need to stay any longer. Stepping with care, he walked out of the cave. He put the bush back in place. Then he headed toward the stream.

It was dark when Dade returned to Cactus's ranch house. He had packed some bread and dried meat with him that morning. It had been gone by noon.

Tired and hungry though he now was, he felt great.

"Cactus," he said, "I think luck is with us."

"What does that mean?" Cactus asked.

"Warm me up some soup, first," Dade said. "Then I'll tell you the whole story."

"It had better be good," Cactus said.

"It's good," Dade said. "It's very good."

Later, Cactus decided that that wasn't the word for it.

"No," he told Dade, "*good* isn't strong enough. I'd say it's the *best* news I've heard in a long time. Maybe in my whole life!"

9

It was almost dark when the stagecoach from Central City pulled in. One man was there to meet it. He stood on the steps of the Red Rock Hotel.

"Hello, Mr. Harper," the driver said to him. "I'm running late today."

"Better late than never," the banker said. He made a dry little smile.

"I guess so," the driver said.

The guard sitting next to the driver reached behind him. "Watch out," he said to Harper. He threw the U.S. mailbag to the ground. Then he jumped down next to it.

"Red Rock!" the guard shouted. "End of the line." He opened the stagecoach door.

A tall, thin man stepped out. He was

dressed all in black. His face was dead white. His dark eyes seemed to shine like black glass.

The man reached back into the coach for his bag. As his coat came open, a flash of white showed. The six-shooter in his holster had a bright bone handle.

Jason Harper took a step toward him. "Mr. Moon?" he asked.

The man in black looked down at the round-faced man before him.

"I'm Simon Moon," he said. His voice was deep.

"How nice to meet you, Mr. Moon," Harper said. He put out his fat little hand. "I'm the man who sent for you. Jason Harper."

Simon Moon took Harper's hand in his. "Hello, Mr. Harper," he said. He looked straight into the banker's eyes. "How long do you think this will take?"

"Oh," Harper said, "not long. You can probably leave on the noon stage tomorrow. I don't think it should take long at all."

Moon's right hand dropped to his holster. "I don't think so, either. One man should be just about a day's work."

Harper's mouth turned down a bit. "Well, Mr. Moon, there *has* been a small change."

"Change?" Moon said. He didn't seem pleased.

"Now," Harper said, "there's another man, too."

"Another man?"

"Please . . . don't worry. You'll be well paid."

Moon didn't answer right away. When he did, his voice was sharp. "The money's only part of it. The time is important, too."

"They'll both be together tomorrow," Harper said. "It should be easy."

"Easy?" Moon said. "Not these things. Fast, sometimes. But never easy."

Harper turned his eyes away. There was something about the way Moon looked at him. It made him feel uneasy. Almost afraid.

Moon spoke. "Do you have a room for me?"

"Oh, yes," Harper said. He turned toward the hotel. "Boy!" he called.

A boy with red hair popped out of the hotel. He ran down the steps two at a time.

Harper took the bag from Moon. He gave it to the boy. "Red, take this to room 23." He handed him a coin.

"Thank you, Mr. Harper," the boy said. He looked in his hand. The coin was a penny. He made a face. Then he carried the bag into the hotel.

Harper took Simon Moon by the arm. "First, Mr. Moon," he said, "let's stop by my office. We can get our business out of the way right now. I know you're not the kind of man who likes to waste time."

Dade and Cactus got an early start. It was a fine morning. Blazer was well rested. So was Lazy Legs. Cactus's little horse had a real spring in his step.

The two men didn't talk much on the ride into Red Rock. They had said what they needed to say back at the ranch.

They hit town about nine o'clock.

As they rode down Main Street, Dade looked around. "That's strange," he said.

"What is?" Cactus asked.

"Where did everyone go?"

It was a good question. Main Street should have been busy by now. It was empty.

"Maybe they all went to church," Cactus said.

Dade gave Cactus a funny look. "On a Tuesday? All of them?"

"Oh. Well, no, I guess not," Cactus said. He rubbed the back of his neck. "I don't keep very good track of time out at the ranch."

Dade brought Blazer to a stop. He held out his hand. "This is far enough," he said. Cactus pulled up on Lazy Legs's reins.

Dade turned in his saddle. He looked up and down the street. He shook his head. There was worry showing on his face.

"Cactus," he said, "I think we need to get a plan together." He pressed his leg against Blazer's side. She turned and moved off toward the side street. Cactus and Lazy Legs followed.

Soon they were inside Danny Flynn's stable.

"Good morning, Danny," Dade said.

"Hello, Dade" the big man said. "I guessed I'd be seeing you today."

"Is that so?"

Danny nodded his head toward Cactus. "Everyone in town knows Cactus Sims is coming to see the sheriff."

"Word gets around fast," Dade said.

"That's right," Danny said. "The trouble is, the sheriff isn't here."

Dade looked surprised.

"No," Danny said. "He left town this morning. Told me he was going to Tom Cleary's."

"But Cleary is supposed to be here!" Cactus said.

"He is," Danny said. "He and his boys rode in about an hour ago. I hear they're down at the hotel talking to Harper and the new man."

"New man?" Dade asked. "What new man?"

Danny looked toward the back of the stable. "Come on out, Red!"

The boy from the hotel stepped forward.

"Go on," Danny said to him. "Tell Mr. Dade about the new man."

"Well" the boy began, "I knew he was a bad man right away. He was mean looking. He has a great big pistol with a bone handle. He . . . tied his holster to his leg. And . . . then I knew. I could see that he . . . he . . ." The boy was tripping over his words.

Dade help up his hand. "Slow down, son!" he said. He climbed down from

Blazer and handed Danny the reins. Then he picked the boy up and set him in the saddle.

"Just take your time," he said. "There's no need for you to rush."

The boy looked down at Dade. His face broke into a wide smile.

"Now," Dade said, "do you think you can tell me the man's name?"

"Yes, sir," the boy said. He was trying his best to speak slowly. "Mr Harper got him a room under the name Jackson. But . . . but . . . ," he started to speed up.

Dade help up his hand.

The boy took a deep breath. He pushed out his chest a little. "But I saw his real name on his bag."

He looked at the three men, his eyes wide.

"Go on, boy," Dade said.

"His real name," the boy almost shouted, "is *Simon Moon!* The famous gunfighter!"

Cactus whistled softly.

"I thought you might want to know about that," Danny said.

"Thanks, Danny," Dade said. "And thank *you*, young man."

Dade lifted the boy and set him down on the ground. Then he took a silver dollar from his pocket and gave it to him. "You go get yourself some candy."

The boy's mouth dropped open. His eyes lit up with joy. It was a lot of money.

Dade felt it was well worth it.

There was no joy in Cactus's eyes. As he got down from Lazy Legs, his look was angry. "So," he said, "they sent Simon Moon after me."

Cactus took a small bag from his shirt pocket. It held bullets for his Sharps buffalo rifle.

"He not after *you*," Dade said. With a quick move, he took the bag from Cactus's hand. "It's me he wants."

"Give me those back!" Cactus barked.

"Sorry," Dade said. He put the bag into his own shirt pocket.

The old man's face grew red. "What do you mean? If they want a fight, I'll give it to them!"

"No, Cactus," Dade said. "You wouldn't stand a chance against Moon."

"But . . ."

"No buts about it, Cactus. Moon is one of the best guns there is."

"The best, is he?" Cactus said. "Well, then, what makes *you* think you can go up against him?"

Dade dug around in his saddlebag. He came out with a rawhide string. "I didn't say he was *the* best."

Cactus watched as Dade tied his holster against his right leg.

"I know you're good," Cactus said. "But you won't be so fast with your paw all banged up."

Dade held up his left hand. "This one works just fine," he said. He opened and closed his fingers. "I'll use a cross-draw. I'll be a hair slow. But not much."

Dade turned the pistol around in the holster. The gun's handle now faced forward.

Cactus shook his head. "Oh, Dade, I don't like this one bit."

"I don't either," Dade answered. "I wish there were another way. But I don't think there is."

He looked at Cactus. "You wait here. I've got to do this by myself."

"All right," Cactus said. But Cactus didn't put a lot of feeling into the words.

Dade walked down the center of Main Street.

About a hundred feet behind him came Cactus. He kept to the side of the street. He hadn't listened to Dade.

Ahead, the street was empty. Along the way, people peeked out of windows.

Mr. Dawson stood in the doorway of his store. Dade nodded to him. He ducked back into the store.

At the end of Main Street, Dade stopped across from the Red Rock Hotel. He cupped his left hand to his mouth. "Simon Moon," he shouted, "come out!"

Dade waited in the empty street.

Suddenly the front door of the hotel opened. Through it stepped Moon, Harper, and Tom and Jed Cleary.

The Clearys and Harper stepped to the side. Moon came down the steps.

He moved out into the street, stopping about 20 feet up from Dade. He wore no coat. The handle of his pistol was bright white in the morning sun.

Dade stood facing Moon. He held his right hand behind his back. His left hand hung by his side.

Moon spoke first. "So, Dade, we finally meet. I've heard a lot about you. You're well known in Texas."

"I've heard about you, too," Dade said.

Moon smiled. It was a cold smile. "Shall we begin?" he said. He held his right hand away from his body.

"Wait!" Dade said. He held his left hand high. "I have something to say first."

Moon nodded. "Go on," he said, "say your piece."

Dade looked at Tom Cleary. "You and Cactus were friends once. Now you're both growing old. You can be friends once more."

"Are you a fool?" Cleary shouted. "He tried to kill my son!"

"No," Dade said. "Not Cactus." He looked Cleary hard in the eye. "Do you remember the gun Cactus always used?"

Cleary thought for a second. "Sure. That Sharps buffalo rifle was his favorite."

"It still is," Dade said. "But that's not the gun that shot your boy. If it had been, Billy would be a dead man now."

"Well, then, who . . . ?" Tom Cleary started to say.

"The same man who found gold in Skull Canyon," Dade said. "The man who tried to buy Cactus out, using your name. The man who killed one of Cactus's longhorns and who shot at him. The man who set you two against each other. The man who tricked the sheriff into leaving town today . . . Jason harper."

"You liar!" Harper shouted. He reached inside his coat. His hand came out gripping a small Derringer pistol. It was pointed right at Dade.

Just as Harper was about to pull the trigger, Jed Cleary stepped forward. With a quick move of his hand, he hit Harper's arm. The bullet went wide. It hit the sign on Dawson's store.

At the same time, Moon made his move.

Dade was ready.

His left hand whipped across his body. In the wink of an eye he had his pistol in his hand. He pulled the trigger once. There was a loud bang.

Simon Moon stepped back with a cry. His pistol dropped to the ground. He gripped his right arm with his left hand. He couldn't believe it.

Dade stepped toward him. He bent over and picked up Moon's pistol. He emptied the bullets out on the ground. Then he stuck it back into Moon's holster.

He looked at Moon's arm. "Doc Jones can look at that. The stagecoach leaves at noon. Be on it!"

Moon said nothing. He turned and walked toward Doc Jones's office.

Dawson rushed out of his store. He had a piece of rope in his hands. "Let's tie this critter up." He made a face at Harper. "We can lock him in the back of my store until the sheriff gets back. I just hope the rats can stand the company."

Jed quickly tied Harper's hands. "Let's go," he said, as he pushed him toward the store.

Dade looked at Cactus and Tom Cleary. "Now," he said, "you two shake hands."

Cactus stuck out his hand first. Cleary was quick to take it. "I guess we have a lot to talk about," he said.

Cactus laughed. "About 25 years to catch up on, I'd say."

Cleary turned to Dade. "Fill me in. How did you know it was Harper?"

"I didn't, at first," Dade said. "It came bit by bit. There was something fishy about Harper's visit to Cactus. He said that you wanted to buy Cactus's ranch, Tom. But it didn't seem you had any need for it. It's a good place for longhorns but not for anything else."

"That's for sure," Cactus broke in.

"And the story about Billy was strange, too. No one but Harper heard Billy say Cactus's name. Harper got away with his lie because Billy couldn't remember anything.

"The pieces didn't really fit together until yesterday. I was poking around in Skull Canyon and I came across an old mine out there. In the mine, I found this."

Dade reached into his shirt pocket. He took out a tiny, flat piece of gold. "There's a lot more where this came from," he said.

"I also found footprints in the mine. It was then that I remembered the first time I met Harper. It was in Peter Dawson's store. Dawson had been sweeping the place out. I noticed that Harper had dried red clay on his shoes. That same clay is on the floor of the Skull Canyon mine."

Dade rubbed his jaw with the back of his hand.

"Harper thought Tom would kill Cactus for killing Billy. When Billy didn't die, Harper decided he'd better come up with a new plan. That's when he sent for Moon."

"And Harper knew I didn't have any family," Cactus said.

"That's right," Dade said. "When you were dead, he'd be able to buy the land cheap. He was going to have Moon take care of me, too."

"How did he know about the mine?" Cleary asked.

"I don't know," Dade said. "As a banker, he may have come across an old claim. I guess that will come out at his trial."

Cactus laughed and banged his hands together. "You sure spoiled his plans!"

"Thank God," Tom Cleary said. "Well," he added, "I've got one more question."

He looked Dade in the eye. "Will you come work for me again?"

"Hold on!" Cactus said. "He works for me! He can run my mine."

"Wait, you two," Dade said. "Don't start fighting again."

Tom Cleary and Cactus looked at each other. They looked at Dade. Then all three men began to laugh.

Dade was still laughing when Dawson came out of the store. He pulled at Dade's arm.

"I forgot to tell you," he said. "This came for you last night." He handed Dade a letter.

Dade looked at the writing on it. He could tell it was from his uncle. As he opened the letter, a smile came to his face.

"This is a nice surprise," Dade said. He took out the check and read it. "It looks like I won't be working for either of you. I'm headed for San Francisco.

Dade put two fingers to his mouth and whistled. As though she'd been waiting for the sound, Blazer came running.

She looked fresh and lively. She looked ready to start the long trip west.

Bad Luck Gold

Janice Greene

1

If someone had told Tom Ringler that he'd find gold that day, he'd have laughed. And if anyone had said it would be the worst thing that ever happened to him, he'd have laughed even harder.

Early that morning, Tom had been out gathering stones. He wanted to make a bridge across the stream that ran beside the cabin. It had rained the night before, and now the stream was too wide to jump across.

Tom's father and the two hired hands, Juan Vasquez and Frank Sitlow, were still in the cabin. They were finishing their morning coffee before starting the day's work. Tom hurried so he'd be ready when they were. Walking down the hill from the cabin, he spotted a good-sized flat rock for the bridge. He lifted it up and suddenly stopped still, staring at the ground. Under the rock were two gold nuggets! He dropped the stone, nearly hitting his foot. He picked up the nuggets and looked at them closely. Could they really be gold? He wondered. "Pa!" he yelled. "Frank! Juan! Come on out here!"

Pa hurried down the hill, his coffee cup still in his hand. Behind him were Juan and Sitlow.

Pa said, "What is it, son?"

"Just look at this," said Tom. He held out his hand.

"Gold!" said Sitlow. He grabbed the nuggets from Tom's hand.

Pa gave Sitlow a hard look. "Let's have the nuggets, Sitlow," he said. He turned to Tom. "Where did you find these, son?" he asked.

Tom showed him. All at once, the men began looking for more gold. Tom and Pa grabbed handfuls of rock and dirt and searched through them. Juan walked quickly up and down the hill, looking under large stones. Sitlow dug through the dirt like a hungry animal. His face turned gray with dust.

The men forgot about the work that was waiting for them. They searched up and down the stream. Tom found one more nugget, a small one. Sitlow found two nuggets. One of them he dropped in his boot while Pa was talking to Tom. The other he gave to Pa with a smile. "Guess it's your lucky day, Mr. Ringler," he said.

"This is good luck for you, señor," said Juan. "The gold will buy you many cows."

Pa grinned. Juan knew that someday he wanted to turn his land into a cattle ranch. Pa looked up at the sun. "It's just about noon already," he said. "We'd better get to work on the barn, so those cows won't have to spend the winter out in the snow. And Tom, you go see to the horses."

Tom gave the horses fresh water, fed them, and joined the other men out at the barn. He worked fast, putting up the boards and hammering them in place with a few quick blows. He couldn't believe how lucky they were, finding gold on their land. They had found the four nuggets so easily. That meant there must be plenty more, waiting to be dug out of the ground.

The gold could make a big difference for him and Pa. It had been a hard life for them in recent months. They had moved

out West a year ago, in 1857. The money
they'd brought with them hadn't gone very
far. Since gold had been discovered in the
mountains, many miners had come to live
here. There weren't enough supplies to go
around, so people had to pay a lot for
them. The high prices had nearly eaten
up Pa's money.

Now maybe he and Pa wouldn't have to
worry so much about the cost of nails or
oats for the horses or food for everyone.
They could hire more men. Juan and
Sitlow helped, especially Juan, who
worked fast and never complained. But
with a few more men, they could finish
the barn in no time. And they could buy
cattle. Tom closed his eyes and saw the
meadow in front of the cabin dotted with
fat brown cattle. The gold was the best
thing that had ever happened to them. At
last they'd had some good luck!

After they had worked for a few hours,
Pa came up to Tom and put a hand on
his shoulder. "Time for a rest, son," he
said. He jerked his head toward the
stream. Tom knew Pa wanted to talk to
him alone.

They walked to the stream and sat
down, leaning back against a couple of

trees. For a while, they listened to the stream in silence. "I guess you were pretty excited about finding the gold," said Pa. "I was myself. But you should have kept quiet and told me about it later. Gold is kind of a test for people. It shows how good or how bad they are. I think it's going to show us that Frank Sitlow can't be trusted."

"Sitlow?" said Tom. "Sitlow's okay, isn't he?"

Pa said, "Didn't you see his face when he caught sight of that gold in your hand?"

"Yes, but . . ."

Pa smiled, but his eyes were sad. "You never see anything but the good in people, Tom," he said. "But I've had my eye on Sitlow for a couple of weeks now. I think he's cheating us. Remember the last time he went to Jim McBain's store for supplies? He came back with hardly anything. He told me prices were high. But I think he sold some of our supplies to the men in the mining camp."

"But Gristy's at the mining camp," Tom said. "He would have heard about it. He would have let us know if Sitlow was cheating us."

Pa's voice was angry. "Maybe Gristy's too busy getting rich," he said.

Tom sighed. He knew that Bill Gristy was like a rock in Pa's boot. Gristy had come out West with the Ringlers. Together he and Pa had settled here in the valley. They built the cabin and hoped to start a cattle ranch someday. When Tom's mother died of Rocky Mountain spotted fever, Gristy became like a second father to him. But several months ago, gold was discovered in the nearby mountains. And Gristy got bitten, as Pa said, "by the gold bug." He went off to live in the mining camp, talking about how he was going to strike it rich. Tom and Pa hadn't seen him since.

CHAPTER

2

The next morning Juan and Sitlow were out feeding the horses. So Tom and Pa looked through the supplies they kept at the back of the cabin.

Pa pointed to the sacks of flour. "Last time Sitlow went to the store, he came back with ten pounds. Didn't you buy fifteen pounds for the same money the time you went?"

Tom nodded.

"And coffee—didn't you buy about five pounds on your last trip?"

Tom nodded again. Sitlow had spent the same money and come back with only two. They looked through the supplies of salt, dried meat, and beans. Tom saw that Sitlow must have cheated them. He could hardly believe it.

The door to the cabin swung open and Sitlow walked in. "Tom, that little gray horse of yours is going to need a new shoe pretty soon," he said. He stopped short as he saw Tom and Pa bent over the supplies. Tom stared at Sitlow's face. The man looked guilty.

Pa turned to Sitlow. "Tom and I were just looking at the supplies you bought. I don't think there's enough to show for the money you spent."

Sitlow didn't look Pa in the face. "Like I told you before, Mr. Ringler, prices just shot up this month."

"I don't think prices rose this much," said Pa. "I think there are folks in the mining camp eating food that I paid for. And I think their money is in your pocket!"

"You've got no right to call me a cheat without any proof!" said Sitlow.

"All right," said Pa. "Suppose we both go to Jim McBain's store down at the south fork tomorrow. Then we'll see what kind of prices he has."

"Suppose you find yourself another hired hand, mister! I've had enough of you anyway. You work a man until he's beat, and then hardly pay him anything!"

"I'll gladly find a man who won't complain every time he does a half hour's work!" said Pa. "You can pack up and leave tomorrow."

"Soon as I get my money," said Sitlow. "You owe me for two months."

"The money you got from the miners is good for one month," said Pa. "I'm sure you charged them plenty. And the nugget you put in your boot yesterday is good for another."

Sitlow looked surprised. Then he turned and stormed over to the other end of the cabin. Sitlow rolled up his two blankets, shoved his deck of cards in his pocket, and put on his gun belt and heavy jacket. Nobody said anything. Sitlow walked out to the corral to get his horse. A few minutes later Tom and Pa heard him ride away.

Tom said, "You'll need to find another hired hand, now."

"I'm looking forward to it," said Pa. "This time I'll find someone who won't steal from me every time my back is turned."

It was already dark when Frank Sitlow finally reached Henry Waybur's saloon. He took his horse to the barn at the back of the place, and then walked inside.

The saloon was crowded full of men. "Hey, Sitlow!" a voice called out. It was Jack Kelly, a man who came to Waybur's saloon almost every night. He was sitting with several other men Sitlow knew. "Pull up a chair, Sitlow," said Kelly. "Ringler give you the night off?"

"I've seen the last of Ringler," said Sitlow. "He's going to have to find himself a new man to push around!" He sat down and told the men what an awful boss Ringler was. It made Sitlow feel a lot better.

Then one of the men said, "Say, isn't that Yuba Jack who just came in?"

Everybody stared at the door. Sitlow needed just one quick look. It *was* Yuba Jack. There was no mistaking the man's nose. It was nearly flat against his face. Sitlow had a cold feeling deep in his stomach, as if he'd swallowed ice. He turned to Kelly. "I've got to go," he said.

Kelly looked surprised, but Sitlow had no time to explain. He got up from the table and stood behind some men who were taller than he was. He watched Yuba

Jack walk slowly through the crowd. Then Sitlow began to work his way toward the door. He thought he could slip outside while Yuba Jack's back was turned. When Yuba Jack bent down to talk to a man at a table, Sitlow saw his chance. He almost ran out the door.

Sitlow walked around the corner of the building and hid there for a minute. He waited to see if anyone came out the door. No one did, so he walked quickly to the barn.

Inside the barn it was as dark as the bottom of a hole. Sitlow felt his way along the wall, moving slowly. All at once he stopped. He could hear someone breathing. He stood perfectly still, listening. He was sure it was Yuba Jack. He thought of running to his horse and riding away quickly. But he was afraid to move. "Let Yuba Jack make the first move," he thought.

Several minutes went by. A horse moved slowly in the dry straw, and then the barn was quiet again. Suddenly, the sound of someone breathing changed to a snore. Sitlow closed his eyes and leaned back against the wall. He felt like laughing. One of Henry Waybur's customers was spending the night in the barn instead of taking the long ride home.

Sitlow walked to the horses and found his own. He thought he'd ride a little way back on the trail and then spend the night hidden in the trees. It would be a long, cold night. But at least he'd be staying away from Yuba Jack. Sitlow swung up on his horse and gave it a kick. The horse jerked its head but didn't move. "What . . . ?" said Sitlow.

There was a noise in the dry straw, and a dark figure came up to him. He heard the click of a gun.

Sitlow's chest felt tight. He knew who it was before the man spoke. "You can forget about going anywhere," said Yuba Jack's deep voice. "I tied your horse's feet."

Sitlow didn't say anything. Behind him, the sleeping man snored peacefully.

"I've been looking for you," said Yuba Jack. "Ever since that night in Claytonville, at the Gold Nugget Saloon. You remember that night, don't you, Sitlow?"

It had been over a year ago, but Sitlow remembered that night very well. There were stairs at the back of the saloon which led to some upstairs rooms. One night Sitlow was sitting on the stairs, counting what little money he had left after a night on the town. Suddenly Yuba Jack came up the stairs in a hurry. He leaned close to Sitlow's face and said, "If a couple of miners come looking for Yuba Jack, you haven't seen him. Got that?" Sitlow nodded and said, "Right. I haven't seen him." Sitlow didn't know Yuba Jack well, but he knew he wasn't a man to argue with. Then Yuba Jack ran up the stairs and disappeared into the first room.

A few moments later, two men came up the stairs, looking for Yuba Jack. Sitlow wasn't going to tell them anything. But then one of the men took a leather bag out of his pocket. Inside was a small gold nugget. Sitlow was nearly broke. The nugget looked just too good to pass up. He told the men where Yuba Jack had gone. He thought he'd never see him again. But now the man was here—holding a gun on him!

"I never said anything to those men!" said Sitlow. "I tell you, I didn't!"

"Don't waste your breath lying, Sitlow," said Yuba Jack. "I heard you. I was on the roof that night, and I heard what you said!"

"So that's where he went!" thought Sitlow. All this time, he'd never known how Yuba Jack had escaped. After searching through all the rooms, the miners had given up. And they had forced Sitlow to give back the nugget, saying he'd been lying.

"So what am I going to do with you now?" said Yuba Jack in a low, ugly voice. "I'm not sure rats like you should be allowed to live."

Sitlow was silent. He was very scared. Then he remembered Ringler's gold. "Listen!" he said. "The man I was working for found gold on his land. A lot of gold. In just one day, we found four nuggets. We hardly had to look for them. I've got one in my pocket—I'll show you!" He pulled out the gold nugget he'd found the day before. Yuba Jack lit a match and looked closely at it. "Not bad," he said.

Sitlow said, "He's got a cabin way out in the woods. There are only three of them out there—him, his kid, and a hired hand. We could go out there, take over the cabin, and keep the gold for ourselves. I'll show you where it is."

"You'll *tell* me where it is," said Yuba Jack. "And I'll ride out there tomorrow and see if your story is true. Wilson can keep you company while I'm gone." He walked over to the sleeping man and gave him a kick. "Wilson," he said. "Get up. There's someone I want you to meet."

The next morning Tom left the cabin to gather wood. He rode his horse Timber out across the stream into the trees. Soon he found a tree that had fallen, and he began to cut it into pieces. Tom liked being alone in the woods. The only sounds he could hear were the calling of birds and the noise of the ax as it cut through the log. All at once Timber snorted loudly. Tom stopped cutting. Timber only snorted like that when there was another horse nearby. Tom looked all around—he saw nothing but trees. Then he looked again and saw something brown moving behind the leaves.

A man on a big buckskin horse rode silently into view. The first thing Tom noticed about the man was his nose. It was almost flat against his face, as if it had been smashed. Except for his nose, the man looked like many of the men Tom had seen out West. He was lean and tan, with sand-colored hair and a light beard.

"Hey!" Tom called. "Hello!" He waved. But the man was gone. Tom stared at the trees a long time. The man had appeared and disappeared so quickly it was as if Tom hadn't seen him at all. It gave him a strange feeling.

Tom finished cutting up the log and tied the pile of wood onto Timber's back. Then he quickly walked his horse back to the cabin. When he got there, Tom told Pa about the strange man he'd seen. Pa became angry, and a worried look crossed his face.

"I don't like seeing strangers around here," he said. "It makes me think Sitlow told some friends of his about our gold. I'm not sure what we can do about it, except keep our guns loaded. I've heard of people doing crazy things to protect their gold. Heard a story about a miner who kept his nuggets in a wooden box. And he put a pair of rattlesnakes in with them."

"Is that the truth, Pa?"

"So they say." Pa shook his head. "I don't know if finding this gold is going to be good luck or bad. Sometimes I think it could land us in a lot of trouble."

"But think of it, Pa," said Tom. "We could hire more men to help with the barn.

And we could buy all the cattle we wanted. It's got to be the best thing that ever happened to us."

"I sure hope you're right, son," Pa said. "But I've been thinking, the sooner we put a claim on that gold, the better. How would you like to make a trip down to Claytonville to file a claim? I'd go myself, but I've got too much to do down here."

Tom had never taken such a long trip on his own. And he was excited. "I'd like it just fine," he said.

Early the next morning, Tom was ready to go. Timber stood waiting. In the saddlebags were bread, dried meat, oats for Timber, and a gold nugget to buy supplies with.

"Keep your fires small, señor," said Juan.

Tom nodded. It wasn't a good idea to build a big fire when you were alone in the mountains. The mountains had once been Indian land. Even though the miners were pushing them out, a few bands of Indians still rode the mountain trails. And if they came across white people, they would sometimes attack. If a man rode alone, he didn't have much of a chance.

"Be careful, son," said Pa. "And don't forget to see about a shoe for Timber when you get to Claytonville."

"I'll do that," said Tom. "See you in a couple of days."

Tom set out across a meadow. Soon he came to the end of the valley and began to climb. The land changed from flat grassland to the rough side of a mountain.

All day Tom rode through the mountains. When the sun was about to set, he found a place to camp near the trail. Then he built a small fire and ate. When he finished his dinner, he cleaned his plate and spread out his blanket. Then he watched the sky slowly change from gold to black.

The next day, Tom followed the trail to the top of the last mountain. He pulled Timber to a stop and looked down through the trees. Below was Claytonville. He couldn't believe the size of it. At the south fork, there were just two buildings—Jim McBain's store and Henry Waybur's saloon. But Claytonville had rows of stores, and streets between them. Wide roads led out of town in all directions, like spokes on a giant wheel. Tom knew one of the roads was used by the stagecoach. It carried mail and shipments of gold.

A while later, Tom stopped Timber and again looked down through the trees at Claytonville. There were people everywhere. Some were on horses. Others were walking along the wooden sidewalks, or coming out of stores. He could read the name of one store. It was called "Callahan's."

In a few minutes, he'd be down the mountain and into town. He shook Timber's reins. "Let's go, boy," he said.

Kate Callahan was standing behind the counter, cutting cloth for a customer when the young man came in. He looked dusty and tired. But when he saw her, he took off his hat and smiled. He had a nice smile, she decided. All at once she was glad she was wearing her favorite dress.

She folded the cloth and handed it to the customer. Kate looked over at the stranger. He was looking right at her, smiling. She smiled back and felt her face turn red.

It was his turn. He needed flour, beans, rope, dried meat, nails, and a frying pan. She gathered the things he wanted and laid them on the counter.

"I see this store is called Callahan's," he said. "Are you Miss Callahan?"

"My name is Kate Callahan."

"I'm Tom Ringler."

She liked his voice. Many of the men who came to Claytonville sounded rough and rude. But he sounded gentle.

"Is this your first visit to Claytonville, Mr. Ringler?"

"Yes, it is," said Tom. "I'll tell you the truth, miss. I've never seen such a town since I came West."

"It is a big place," she said. "There's a post office, a doctor, and a restaurant— the Stage House. That's that big building across the street. There's a jail, too. The county sheriff, Mr. Bell, lives here. And the stagecoach comes through every two weeks. Do you live around here, Mr. Ringler?"

"I live in the next county," he said. "My Pa and I have a cabin just above the south fork of the Fallon River."

"You're not a miner, are you, Mr. Ringler?" she asked.

He smiled. "Is that so easy to see, Miss Callahan?"

"I guess it's because you sound like you're happy with what you have," she said. "People digging for gold always sound like they're hungry for more."

"Well, in a way, I do want more," Tom said. "Pa and I want to own a cattle ranch someday."

"That sounds like a good thing to want," she said.

He began to gather up his supplies. She was sorry he lived so far away. "I hope you'll be coming to Claytonville again sometime, Mr. Ringer."

"I certainly hope to, Miss Callahan," he said with a smile.

Kate's face turned red again. But his smile made her feel pretty, and warm inside.

Tom read the sign outside the Stage House: DINNER $3. He shook his head. Three dollars for a meal! But since this was the only restaurant in town, he went in.

After Tom ate, he went to the claims office. There he signed several papers. They gave him and Pa the rights to any gold they had found—and would find on their land in the future. He walked out of the office whistling. Now the gold belonged to the Ringlers for as long as they lived. He walked to where Timber was tied up in front of a saloon. He folded the claim papers carefully. Then he put them in his saddlebag along with the supplies he had bought at Callahan's store.

Tom swung himself up in the saddle, shook the reins, and headed Timber toward the end of town. As he passed Callahan's store, he looked through the open door. He was hoping to see Kate inside, but he couldn't. He wished he had time to see her again. But he had a lot of trail to ride before dark.

It wasn't until he was deep in the mountains that Tom suddenly remembered Timber's shoe. He'd forgotten all about it. He checked the shoe and found that one of the six nails had fallen out. Another one seemed loose. The shoe could hang on for days, or it could come off in the next hour. Anyway, Tom knew he'd better take it slow for the rest of the trip. If Timber threw a shoe on a rough mountain trail, he could have a bad fall.

Tom rode the trails carefully, never hurrying his horse. Often, he thought of Kate. He remembered her voice, and her hands, which were small but looked strong. She had seemed so friendly and helpful. He thought he'd like to make a return trip to Claytonville soon.

It was late the following afternoon when Tom rode through the meadow toward the cabin. He looked for Pa at the barn, but he couldn't find him. He must have quit early, Tom decided.

Then Tom noticed the four extra horses in the corral. One of the horses was a big buckskin. Tom thought it was odd for Pa to have so many visitors. He looked over at the cabin and pulled Timber to a stop. The wooden door was smashed, as if someone had kicked it open. Tom's skin went cold.

"Pa!" he called out.

4

Tom heard footsteps inside the cabin. Then a voice rang out, "It's Ringler's boy!" The door opened. The man with the flattened nose aimed his gun. Tom ducked. The shot buzzed over his back. He slapped Timber's side and the horse took off.

Tom flew across the meadow, heading back toward the mountains. Behind him he could hear shouts and the sound of the corral gate being opened. They were coming after him.

If he could just reach the mountains, Tom thought. He could lead Timber off the trail and hide among the rocks. Then he remembered Timber's loose shoe. "Better not take a chance in the mountains," he thought.

Tom felt trapped. Should he let Timber go, he wondered, and hide in the meadow grass? No, he decided. He'd be a sitting duck, hiding so close to the cabin. Where could he go? The stream? It was close, and there were plenty of trees to hide in. He turned Timber toward the stream.

For more than an hour, Tom led his horse down the stream. When it began to get dark, he looked for a place to spend the night. He found a spot where the trees and brush were thick. He led Timber into the hiding place. Then he cut down a bush and dragged it across the tracks they had made, walking from the stream to the trees.

Tom sat down near Timber, leaned against a tree, and closed his eyes. He was tired and hungry. He took a piece of dried meat from the saddlebags and ate it slowly He wondered what had happened at the cabin while he was in Claytonville. He wondered if Pa and Juan were all right.

Timber snorted. Tom held his breath and listened. He heard the sounds of twigs breaking and horses walking over the soft ground. He stood up silently and patted Timber's neck. "Quiet, Timber," he whispered. "Quiet now, boy." He could hear the riders come closer. Slowly, he drew his gun.

Timber stamped his hoof. Tom held his breath.

"Hey! Hold up a minute!" Tom knew the voice. It was Frank Sitlow's.

"What's up?" said a deep voice.

"Didn't you hear a horse?" said Sitlow. "Sounded like his horse."

"Sounded like *your* horse, Sitlow," said another voice.

"Shut up, Wilson," said the man with the deep voice.

There was no sound except for the light wind through the trees. Tom stood waiting, his hand on his gun. Several long moments passed.

Wilson broke the silence. "Let's go back," he said. "It's getting dark and it looks like there won't be a moon tonight. Pretty soon we won't be able to see our hands in front of our faces."

"We're not even sure if he went this way," Sitlow said.

"Shut up, you two," said the deep voice.

The riders started back down the stream. Tom waited until he couldn't hear them. Then he rolled out his blanket, lay down between two trees, and slept.

He woke up just as the sky was turning light. His body felt stiff and cold. And his heart was bitter. He thought about Sitlow. The man had often been kind to him. When it was his turn to cook breakfast, he always made pancakes, which Tom loved. "Got to give the kid his favorite," Sitlow would say.

Tom had always thought Sitlow was a good man. But Sitlow had cheated his father, maybe even killed him. And Sitlow had almost gotten Tom killed, too. "If I die," Tom thought, "the claim in my saddlebag isn't worth anything."

Tom put his head in his hands, wondering what to do. He had never felt so alone. Then he thought of Bill Gristy. Gristy would help him! He was always ready to take charge of things. And he was quick and sure with a gun.

The problem was reaching Gristy at the mining camp. Tom was afraid to take the trails through the mountains. Many people used them, and he was afraid he would be seen. Maybe he could make it through the mountains without using the trails. It was worth a try.

Tom headed out right after he had breakfast. He cut sideways across the meadow. Looking back in the direction of the cabin, he saw no one. Soon the meadow grass changed to dry brush and rock. He began to climb. It was a hard way to go. Often, bushes or rocks were piled up high and he had to lead Timber around them.

It was almost dark by the time Tom reached the mining camp. As he rode slowly along the road to the camp, he spotted a miner working on a hill a little way up from the road. Tom got down from Timber and walked toward the man. The miner was bent over a pile of wet rocks and dirt. He was picking through the pile, looking for nuggets.

Tom's foot slipped a little coming up the hill. The man jumped at the sound and whirled around to face Tom. He had his gun in his hand.

"Whoa!" Tom put his hands in the air. "I didn't mean any harm, mister."

"Prove it," said the man.

"I'm looking for Bill Gristy," said Tom. "And my gun's back there with my horse."

The miner slowly lowered his gun. "Well, you shouldn't come sneaking up on folks like that," he said. "You're asking for a bullet when you do."

"I'll remember that," said Tom. "You know where I can find Bill Gristy?"

The miner pointed a dirty finger. "That little tent just down the road on the right. He'll be there. He always is, these days."

"What's the matter," said Tom. "Is he sick?"

"You'll see for yourself," said the miner. He turned away and went back to his pile of rocks.

Bill Gristy lay on his blanket, staring into space. He was hungry, but his leg hurt and he didn't feel strong enough to get up. He thought of the wife and three children he had left behind in the East. He hadn't had a letter from them in a long time. He wished he were back East with them. Instead he was lying here, cold, broke, and hungry, in this dirty mining camp.

When gold was discovered in these mountains, Gristy had had dreams of striking it rich. He'd worked like a dog, digging the earth until he thought his back would break. He found a few nuggets, but he had to use them to buy food. Then, for a long time, he didn't find any gold at all. Now he was stuck in this camp, where so many men died from sickness, or from greed for another man's gold.

Tom poked his head into Gristy's tent. It was dark and smelly inside. "Gristy?" he called softly.

Gristy groaned as he sat up. "Tom Ringler? That you, boy?"

"It's me," said Tom.

"Come on over here where I can see you," said Gristy. "You look older, Tom. Not like a kid anymore."

"Gristy, are you all right?" Tom asked. Gristy looked as if he hadn't eaten in a week, or had a bath in a month.

"Not so good, Tom," said Gristy. "I had a pretty bad fall a couple of weeks ago. Hurt my leg. I can get around okay now, but to tell the truth, I've been felling pretty low. You know all those plans I had for getting myself a pile of gold. Well, they didn't work out so well. But let's hear about you. How's that Pa of yours?"

Suddenly Tom felt like crying. He looked away. "I don't know, Gristy. I don't know if he's alive." He told Gristy the story of Sitlow being fired, and the stranger with the flattened nose he had seen. He also told him about the trip to Claytonville, and what had happened the day he came back.

Gristy shook his head sadly. "I sure liked your Pa, Tom. He was a fine man."

"Well, don't bury him yet!" said Tom in an angry voice.

"Sorry, Tom."

"It's all right," Tom said sadly. They sat in the dark tent. Tom's stomach felt hollow. "Do you have anything to eat?" he asked.

"There might be some dried meat in that coat over there," said Gristy.

Tom had been eating dried meat for two days. "Where can I get some food around here?" he asked.

"Well, one of the miners might sell you something."

"Sounds good," said Tom. "I think we both could use a good meal."

"That would be fine, Tom, really fine," said Gristy. "I haven't been up to feeding myself much lately."

Tom walked quickly out of the tent. His hope was slipping away. He had tried so hard to reach Gristy, but it seemed he had come to a dead end. How could Gristy help him when he wouldn't even fix himself a meal?

When Gristy shared the land with Pa, he used to be the first one up in the morning. Before sunrise, when it was still dark and cold, Gristy used to yank Tom's blanket off. "You going to sleep all day, boy?" he'd yell. "Better get up before it's noon!" Now Gristy was like a sick old man.

Down the road, Tom spotted a miner shoveling wet rocks and dirt into a wooden box. "Evening," said Tom.

"Evening," said the man. He kept on shoveling.

"I was wondering if you had any food I could buy," asked Tom.

"Buy your own," the man said in a low voice as he bent over his work.

"What's that?" asked Tom.

"I said, 'buy your own.' Every time I go down to the store, some thief starts digging for my gold. I'm keeping my food, and you get your own."

Tom turned and walked away. He walked about a half a mile, passing several miners. The men were bent over shovels or picking through boxes of rock and dirt with their hands. They looked up at Tom as he passed, and then turned back to their work.

Then Tom heard someone whistling. He followed the sound until he found a miner washing his shirt in a creek. "Evening," said the man as Tom walked up. The man's hair and beard were almost white, but his face looked young.

"Evening," said Tom. "I wonder if you have any food I could buy?"

The man grinned. "That I do," he said. "Sam Dodson's the name." He wiped a hand on his pants and stuck it out to Tom.

Tom shook it. "Tom Ringler," he said.

"Well, follow me, Mr. Ringler." He led Tom to a tiny cabin. There Tom bought eggs, fresh meat, and potatoes.

"I'm sorry to take your money," said Dodson. "I'd feel better if I could just give you the food. But it's been a long time since I've seen any gold. I'm pretty broke right now."

"It's all right," said Tom. But to himself, Tom said, "I'll bet you're as greedy as the rest, Dodson. You just talk sweeter."

CHAPTER

5

Tom began making dinner for himself and Gristy. Soon, the good smell of eggs and potatoes filled the tent. Tom was about to dish up the meal when a big man in a torn buckskin jacket stepped inside.

"Smells just fine," said the man. "Lucky I happened to be passing by."

Tom looked at Gristy. "He a friend of yours?" he asked.

Gristy shrugged. "I've seen him around," he said.

"There isn't enough for you," said Tom.

"Then you'll just have to give up your share, kid," said the man with an ugly grin. "I'm hungry, and I aim to eat!"

"Go ahead and give him some, Tom," said Gristy. "It isn't worth fighting over."

Tom felt like hitting the stranger. But he was tired and hungry, and the man was a lot bigger than he was. And he knew if he fought the stranger, he wouldn't get any help from Gristy.

Tom dished out an extra plate of food. The man bent over the plate and didn't look up until he was finished. He wiped his mouth with his hand, got up, and left.

Tom couldn't look Gristy in the eye. It made him angry that Gristy let himself get pushed around. He was mad at himself, too, for not standing up to the stranger.

Later, Tom moved aside some of Gristy's clothes, a wooden box, and a shovel, to make room for his blanket.

"Sorry there isn't much room," said Gristy. "Maybe we can clean up a little tomorrow."

"If you want to clean the place up, you can take a bath," said Tom. "Smells too strong for a skunk in here."

"You don't smell so sweet yourself, kid," said Gristy. "So you get the first dip in the creek tomorrow. And I'm telling you, it's not exactly warm."

Lying in the dark, Tom grinned. That was the way Gristy used to talk.

The next day, Tom and Gristy had breakfast and then took a cold swim in the creek. After they cleaned up the tent, Tom said, "Let's do a little target shooting."

"I don't know, Tom," said Gristy. "Maybe I ought to just take it easy, with this leg."

"Maybe you've been so busy digging for gold you aren't so good anymore," said Tom with a grin. "Maybe you're afraid I'm a better shot than you now."

Gristy gave Tom a look. "Smart-mouth kid," he said. He put on his gun belt.

They walked out to an open space. Gristy walked slowly, dragging his bad leg. Tom threw rocks high in the air and Gristy shot at them. He hardly missed any. Then Gristy threw rocks for Tom. Tom wasn't anywhere near as good, and he knew it. But he knew he made Gristy look even better.

"You're great," said Tom. "You're the fastest draw and the best shot in the whole county, I bet."

"Anybody would look good, next to you," said Gristy. But Tom knew he felt proud.

Tom tried to act cheerful around Gristy. But every time he thought about his Pa, he felt a deep pain inside. He hoped somehow that Pa and Juan had managed to escape. But he knew there wasn't much chance of that.

That night after supper, Tom said, "What do you think about you and me going after Sitlow and those other men?"

"I don't think much of the odds. It would be four of them against two of us."

"What if I gave you half the gold on my land?" said Tom.

"You don't have to buy me, kid," said Gristy angrily.

"Sorry," said Tom. "I didn't, I don't know . . ."

"Don't you think people do anything for free?" said Gristy. "You've changed a lot, kid."

"I guess I have," said Tom. He thought that since Pa had fired Sitlow, he'd learned to see the worst side of people.

"Tom," said Gristy. "I care a lot about your Pa. And I'm going to do all I can for him. Why don't we go out to that saloon at the south fork tomorrow and see if we can find out any news? Or maybe I'd better go alone, seeing as how those men are looking for you."

"Sounds good to me," said Tom. "I'd like any kind of news. I hate not knowing what happened."

"I don't blame you, son. I feel the same way."

Tom was sitting in front of the tent carving a piece of wood when Gristy returned. He had food and a lot of news.

Gristy said, "That fellow with the flat nose you saw—he's called Yuba Jack. Folks say he cheated a couple of miners out of their claims. He took all the gold for himself. And some people say he was one of the men who robbed the Claytonville stagecoach back in the spring. But nobody's been able to prove it."

Tom kept on carving. He could tell Gristy had more to say.

"I've got some bad news, too, kid," said Gristy slowly. "I heard Yuba Jack was in a gunfight a couple of days back. Two men were killed—a settler and his hired hand. I'm sure sorry to have to tell you this, Tom."

Tom cut a long, ugly mark across the wood with his knife. He got up quickly and walked away. He walked out of the mining camp up into the trees. He hardly saw where he was going. He had tried to be ready for the news of Pa's death. But when it came, it hit him hard.

Nothing had ever hurt him this much. And nothing had made him this angry. When his mother had died, it had been from sickness. They hadn't been able to help her. But his Pa and Juan had been killed on purpose. And now Tom wanted more than anything to get even.

Finally, when he was hungry and tired from walking, Tom came back to the tent. Gristy was fixing dinner, moving quickly in spite of his bad leg.

"I think it's time to get moving, Tom," he said. "Let's go down to the saloon at the south fork tonight. We'll see if we can't get a couple of men to help us go after Yuba Jack and the others."

Tom nodded. "I don't feel like letting them go free another day," he said.

That night after supper, Tom and Gristy went down to Henry Waybur's saloon. When they arrived, they found the place bright and noisy. Tom and Gristy stood inside the door, looking around the room. "Let's have a word with those men at that corner table," said Gristy. "They're miners I've seen around."

He led Tom across the room to the four men who were playing cards.

"Evening, boys," said Gristy. "If you don't mind, I'd like just a few minutes of your time."

"Well, make it short," said a red-faced man. "I'm just about to win this hand."

Gristy told the men about Yuba Jack and his men killing Tom's Pa and Juan Vasquez. "So how about you fellows joining us?" said Gristy. "He's got four men. If we have six, it shouldn't be that hard to bring him in."

"I'll tell you the truth," said one miner. "I hate to go off and leave my claim, even for just a day or two. How about getting the Claytonville sheriff to help you out?"

"He's got his own county to worry about," said Gristy. "Besides, the people up here at the south fork ought to take care of their own business."

"Gristy's getting nowhere," Tom thought. He spoke up, "The reason Yuba Jack—"

The red-faced man broke in, "I don't have all night to listen to some kid! Get lost!"

Tom reached out with his foot and pushed the man's chair leg. The man fell on the floor with a crash. For an instant, the whole saloon was silent. Then the man leaped to his feet with an angry yell. He tried to grab Tom's shirt, but Gristy caught his arm and twisted it. The man's face jerked with pain.

"Easy now, mister," said Gristy. "You're going to sit down nice and quiet and listen to what the kid has to say."

The man sat down, rubbing his arm. He fixed Gristy with an angry stare, but he kept quiet.

"As I was saying," said Tom, "The reason Yuba Jack killed my Pa was to get his hands on our gold. If we don't stop him now, he'll be free to go after other people's claims. Any one of you might be his next target."

"The kid's got a point there," said Gristy. The men nodded.

All the miners except the red-faced man said they would help go after Yuba Jack and his men.

"Meet us in front of the saloon two hours before sunset tomorrow," said Gristy. "Anybody have some empty flour sacks they can bring along?"

"I've got a couple," said one man. "What do you need them for?"

"You'll see," said Gristy. "I've got a plan to chase that rat out of his hole."

When Tom and Gristy walked back to the tent that night, Tom thought about how Gristy had been acting like his old self again. And that was sure good to see. Tom was glad, too, that the miners were going to help them. But Tom was certain that only their fear of losing their gold made them willing to go after Yuba Jack. He said to himself, "You were right, Pa. I used to see only the good in people. And I was a fool."

CHAPTER

6

Tom and Gristy joined the miners in front of Waybur's saloon the next afternoon. Sam Dodson was there with them. "I heard you were going after Yuba Jack," he said. "Thought you might like to have an extra gun."

Tom grinned. "Glad to have you along," he said.

The men rode out toward the cabin. Tom's throat was dry. He wondered what was waiting for them there. When they were about half a mile away, Gristy led them to the stream.

"All right," he said. "Who's got the flour sacks?"

"Here you go," said a miner, handing him the empty sacks.

"Thanks," said Gristy. "Now we're going to get these a little bit wet, but not wet clear through. Then we're going to fill them up with wet leaves. When it's dark, we'll bring them up to the cabin and shove them underneath it. Then we'll set them on fire."

"Won't they burn the cabin?" said Tom.

"They won't burn," said Gristy. "They'll smoke—smoke like crazy."

Two hours later, Sitlow, Wilson, Yuba Jack, and a man named Harlow were playing cards inside the cabin.

"Your turn to draw, Sitlow," said Harlow.

"Hold on," said Yuba Jack in a low voice. "I hear something."

Sitlow listened. There *was* something— or someone—near the door. Then he heard footsteps running away from the cabin, down the hill.

Yuba Jack pushed the door open, aimed, and fired into the night. From out of the trees, three shots fired back. One just missed Yuba Jack's knee.

Yuba Jack slammed the door shut. "Missed him," he said. "And there are at least three more out there."

"Smoke!" said Wilson. "I smell smoke! They're burning the place! We've got to get out of here!"

"Shut up, Wilson," said Yuba Jack. "We'll wait until it's good and smoky. That'll give us some cover. Then we'll make a run for it."

They waited. Gray smoke came up between the floorboards. Sitlow's throat felt as if it were full of cotton. He began to cough. He could hear Harlow coughing across the room, but he could hardly see him.

Finally, Yuba Jack said, "All right. Wilson, you're out the door first. Head straight for the corral. Then Harlow and me. Sitlow, you cover us until we're halfway to the corral. Then you come, too."

"If I go first, they'll pick me off easy," said Wilson. "Let's all go out together. What do you say?"

"Get out there, Wilson," said Yuba Jack. "Or I'll shoot you myself." He opened the door and gave Wilson a shove.

Wilson ran out into the smoky night. Two shots rang out. Sitlow tried to return the fire. But he couldn't see where the shots came from. Harlow and Yuba Jack ran out next. There were more shots, and shouting voices. Sitlow ran out of the cabin. A shot rang out, and he felt the bullet buzz by his chest.

Sitlow heard footsteps nearby. He kept running. His eyes were watery from the smoke. The footsteps came closer. He crashed through the middle of a bush, scratching his hands and face. Suddenly two men were on each side of him. They had guns pointed at his head.

"Don't you make a move now, mister," said a tall man with white hair and a beard. Another man tied Sitlow's hands behind his back. Sitlow stared through the smoke. Something was moving in the corral. Yuba Jack's horse!

"There he is!" someone yelled. "In the corral!"

Yuba Jack jumped his horse over the corral fence. The man with the white beard fired and missed. The horse ran off through the smoke.

The men took Sitlow to the cabin. Harlow and Wilson were already there, their hands tied behind their backs. Wilson had been shot in the shoulder.

Ringler's boy came over to Sitlow. At first Sitlow didn't know who it was. The kid's face was dirty, and his hair was hanging in his eyes. "I want to know what happened to my Pa," he said.

Sitlow stared silently at the floor.

Suddenly, the kid grabbed him by the hair, jerking his head back. "I said, I want to know what happened! You're going to tell me, or I'm going to put a bullet in your leg!"

Sitlow stared at the kid. All the time he was working for Ringler, he had never heard an angry word from the boy. But now the kid's eyes looked as cold and hard as stone.

"Okay, okay," said Sitlow. "Yuba Jack heard about you finding that gold up here. . . ."

"You think I'm stupid, Sitlow?" Tom said. "There was one way Yuba Jack could have heard about the gold—from you!"

"Okay," said Sitlow quickly. "I'm telling you the honest truth now. Yuba Jack had it in for me. So I told him about your gold. I had to—to save my neck! He made me tell him where your place was. We rode out here together, five of us.

"We came to this spot down the hill from the cabin. He just sat there, waiting, until someone came out the door. It was

Vasquez. He never knew what hit him. Yuba Jack called to your Pa to give up, but he wouldn't. He held on just about all night. Then we got the cabin door open. Your Pa got one of us, a fellow by the name of Moore."

"Which one of you killed my Pa?" said Tom.

"It was Yuba Jack," said Sitlow.

Tom leaned over him, his face dark red with anger. "Sure it wasn't you, Sitlow?"

"It was Yuba Jack!" said Sitlow. "I saw him do it! It wasn't me!"

One of the men put his hand on the kid's shoulder. "Sounds like he's probably telling the truth," the man said. He led the kid away. Sitlow felt wet all over with sweat. The kid had looked ready to kill him.

The next morning, three miners left the cabin with Sitlow, Wilson, and Harlow. They were headed for the jail at Claytonville. Tom, Gristy, and Sam Dodson began following the trail of Yuba Jack.

The trail led them out of the valley and up into the mountains. As he rode along, Tom felt a growing hatred for Yuba Jack.

He had never hated anyone before. But now he felt he could easily shoot the man—and smile as he pulled the trigger.

Tom thought about the gold he'd found. He'd felt so lucky at the time. But the gold had shown him how awful people could be. And because of the gold, Juan and Pa had died. Tom thought finding the gold was the worst thing that had ever happened to him.

The trail took them over the mountains to the other side. There the land changed. The rain hardly ever reached this side of the mountains. It was dry and hot here. Looking out over the flat land, Tom couldn't see a single tree.

They followed the trail until the sun went down. Then they stopped for the night and built a fire. Without the sun, the air turned cold very quickly. Gristy cooked a meal of beans.

After dinner, Tom walked off by himself. He thought about how strange it had been to be in the cabin without Pa. He wondered how he could ever go back and live there alone. But he couldn't think of anywhere else to go. Finally, he was too cold and tired to think anymore. He walked slowly back to the camp.

Gristy and Dodson were already laying out their blankets near the fire. Tom wrapped himself up in his blanket, but he couldn't get to sleep. If he lay with one side facing the fire, the other side of him stayed cold.

Sam Dodson got up and laid his heavy jacket over Tom. "I've got a pretty thick blanket," he said. "So you might as well use this jacket of mine."

"Thanks," said Tom. The man's kindness warmed him as much as the jacket. Soon he fell asleep.

The next morning the three men waited until it was light enough to see the tracks from Yuba Jack's horse. Then they began following the trail again. By noon it was hotter than it had been the day before. The sun beat down on the men and their horses. Gristy and Dodson kept looking around for some shade. They needed a cool place to stop for a while. A couple of hours went by. The horses walked slowly, their heads hanging. Then Gristy let out a yell. "Look up ahead! Must be a spring over there!" About a mile away was a small group of trees.

Yuba Jack had wanted to reach the trees, too. His tracks led straight to them.

The horses walked faster. They could smell the water.

The trees at the spring were small and the water was brown. But after the dry, hot land, this was like heaven. The men and horses had a long drink.

"I think we better stay here for at least an hour," said Gristy.

Tom gave him a hard look. "We can't do that," he said. "Suppose a dust storm came up. We'd lose the trail."

"An hour isn't going to hurt us," said Gristy. "I don't like the look of these horses."

"You're crazy!" said Tom. "Yuba Jack's going to be in the next state before we get near him again!"

Gristy grabbed Tom by the arms and shook him. "I'm not talking about Yuba Jack! I'm talking about our horses! Look at that horse of yours. Can you tell me he doesn't need the rest?"

Tom looked at Timber. The horse's eyes were half closed. His gray coat was almost black with sweat. Tom turned away. He felt awful.

Dodson said, "We're going to find him, Tom. Maybe not today or tomorrow. But we're going to get him."

That night after supper, Tom walked away from the campfire. Dodson stepped up beside him. "Mind having some company?" he asked.

"I guess not," said Tom, though he really wanted to be alone.

They walked for a while without speaking. Then Dodson said, "You know, when I came out West, I had a lot of dreams. I was going to find a pile of gold and become a rich man. Now I'm just about ready to give it all up."

"Doesn't anybody get rich finding gold?" asked Tom.

"Oh, some do. When gold was first discovered in the mountains here, one man made $4000 in three days. But nobody's gotten rich since I've been here. I've been working hard for a year, and I'm getting *poorer* every day."

"Sounds rough," said Tom.

"It is, and I'm ready to quit. Tell you what I'd really like to do. I'd like to work on a cattle ranch. That's what I used to do before I came out here."

Tom said, "That's what my Pa and I wanted to do. Now, I don't know."

"Don't give it up," said Dodson. "It's a hard life, but it's a good one."

Tom and Dodson talked for a long time about cattle and how to run a ranch. Tom thought Dodson would make a fine hired hand, maybe even a partner. But he didn't want to trust anyone. Not after Sitlow.

The next day, they had been riding for about an hour when Dodson saw buzzards up ahead. There were five of them, flying in lazy circles in the hot sky.

"Looks like something died," said Dodson.

The trail led them to where the buzzards were circling. They rode up slowly. "Over there," said Gristy.

The buckskin horse was lying on the ground. "She's shot in the head," said Tom when they got closer to the horse. "I wonder what happened?"

"Look at this," said Dodson. The horse's front leg was turned in an odd way.

"She must have stepped in a prairie dog hole and broken her leg," said Gristy.

"Fine looking horse," said Dodson. "Too bad."

"It won't be long now," said Tom. His eyes were bright and hard.

CHAPTER

7

They followed Yuba Jack's trail to a deep, narrow gulch. "This is it, boys," said Gristy. "Yuba Jack knows he can't outrun us. So he's picked this spot to shoot it out. I figure that between the three of us we've got him licked. Dodson, you cover the other side of the gulch, in case he makes a run for it. Tom and I'll go after him from this end."

"Okay," said Dodson. He rode off.

Tom and Gristy walked slowly into the gulch, their guns drawn. There were big rocks everywhere, some of them large enough to hide a couple of men. Every time they came close to a rock, Tom wondered if Yuba Jack were hiding behind it.

"Let's work our way to the left," said Gristy. "Then maybe we can spot him."

They moved to the left, using the rocks as a cover. As they ducked down behind a rock, Gristy grabbed Tom's shoulder. "Look up there," he said in a low voice. "Just between those two square-looking rocks."

Tom looked. There between the rocks, he could see the brown leather of Yuba Jack's boot.

"Now we've got to draw his fire," said Gristy.

"I know how to do that," said Tom. "Sitlow showed me this trick." He took off his hat and stuck it on the end of his gun. Then he raised it up over the rock, so that only the hat showed. Nothing happened.

Tom moved the hat around to draw Yuba Jack's fire. Still nothing happened. "What's the matter with him?" said Tom.

"I think he knows that trick, son. Why don't we both fire at that boot of his. That ought to get him going."

They leaned out from each side of the rock and shot at Yuba Jack's boot. Yuba Jack fired back, hitting the rock next to Tom's head.

Tom and Gristy looked at each other, "Pretty quick, isn't he?" said Gristy.

Tom nodded. Yuba Jack wasn't going to make it easy for them. Several times they drew his fire. The man was quick and deadly with his gun, and bullets flew close to Tom and Gristy.

Gristy called out, "You know you can't last forever up there! Better give up now and save yourself some trouble!"

Yuba Jack called back, "You may get me, but I'm going to kill one of you before I go! Or maybe I'll just kill you all!"

The battle went on. The sun grew cooler and the shadows from the rocks grew long. Tom kept thinking that his father's killer was so close, yet just out of reach. It was driving him crazy. Finally, he said to Gristy, "I can't stand this. I'm going up after him."

Gristy grabbed his arm. "Don't try it, Tom. He's too fast. He'll nail you, sure as I'm sitting here."

Tom jerked his arm out of Gristy's hand. "Cover me," he said.

Keeping low to the ground, he ran to a nearby rock. Yuba Jack's bullets followed him. Tom had his eye on a large rock halfway up the gulch. He began to run toward it. He heard Gristy's gun behind him.

Suddenly a bullet buzzed over his head. The next one would hit him! Tom threw himself on the ground. Then Gristy's hand was on his boot and he was being pulled backward. Gristy dragged him behind a rock.

Tom leaned back against the rock, breathing hard. Then he saw Gristy's hand. "You're bleeding!" he said.

Gristy was tearing a strip of cloth from the sleeve of his shirt. "He got me," Gristy said. "But it's nothing to worry about. You okay?"

"Sure, thanks to you. I guess I made a pretty stupid move."

"You bet you did," said Gristy. "Here, tie this on."

Tom tied the cloth around Gristy's hand. The gulch was silent. Gristy grinned. "I'll bet he's out of bullets," he said.

He called out to Yuba Jack. "You're out of bullets, mister. You know it and we know it. Come out now with your hands up; and we'll take you to the sheriff at Claytonville. That sound better to you than getting shot?"

There was no answer. Gristy's words seemed to hang in the air. Then Yuba Jack rose from behind the rock. He put his hands up and walked slowly toward them.

Tom stared at Yuba Jack, at the tan face and flattened nose. Suddenly, his anger filled him. His father was dead— while this man lived! He aimed his gun at Yuba Jack's chest. But Gristy stepped between them.

"Put your gun down, son," Gristy said. "If you shoot him, you'll be no better than he is. And killing him won't bring your Pa back."

Tom stared at Gristy for a long moment. Then he lowered his gun.

"Come on," said Gristy. "Let's go get Dodson. He must be thinking we died of old age by now."

The trip back from the gulch went faster than the one going there, for they had no trail to follow. By the time they stopped for the night, they had almost made it to the mountains. They had tied Yuba Jack's hands in front of him, so he could ride and eat. He sat at the fire with Tom and

Gristy, waiting for Dodson to finish making a meal of beans.

Tom kept staring at Yuba Jack. It was strange, he thought, to be sitting so close to the man who had killed his father. It was also strange that a killer could sound so warm and friendly.

"I can tell you're all hard-working fellows," Yuba Jack said with a smile. "And I know it's a hard life out here. A man can work until he drops and still barely make enough to feed himself."

"What are you working up to, mister?" said Gristy. "If you're going to say something, say it."

"I just think fellows like you could use a little break," said Yuba Jack. "I've been pretty lucky, myself. Matter of fact, I have about $5000 in gold, hidden up in the mountains. That's a lot of money. There would be more than a thousand for each of us. What do you say to that, fellows?"

Dodson snorted. "I'd say it's a lie," he said.

Yuba Jack shook his head. "I'll take you up there and show you the place I hid it."

"Funny how a man always wants to make a side trip on his way to jail," said Gristy. "I bet there's a couple of your friends near that hiding place. A couple of friends with guns."

"Okay, don't believe me," said Yuba Jack. "I'll tell you, though, you're missing out on a lot of money."

"It's time to quit talking and start eating," said Dodson, dishing up the beans.

Yuba Jack ate like a wild animal. He looked around after each quick bite. It was as if he wanted to make sure nobody was going to take the food away from him. When he was finished, he said. "That's fine cooking, Mr. Dodson. I'll have a little more if you don't mind."

"That's all you're getting," said Dodson. "You're lucky to get any at all."

Yuba Jack shook his head slowly. "It's a sad thing when people can't spare a hungry man a little food," he said.

"They'll fatten you up plenty in jail," said Gristy.

Yuba Jack was quiet for a moment, and then he turned to Tom. "You're awfully quiet, kid," he said.

"Don't have anything that needs to be said," Tom answered.

Yuba Jack said, "I've been wondering if you know how well off you are."

Tom said nothing. His face was blank.

"That land of yours has gold on it, a lot of gold. I've seen it myself. You could be a rich man, if you play your cards right. But you've got to be extra careful. People are going to act like they're your friends. But they'll just be waiting for a chance to get their hands on your gold. Now these two so-called friends of yours—"

Gristy jumped to his feet and shoved his fist close to Yuba Jack's face. "You shut your mouth, or I'll shut it for you!" he shouted.

"Gristy!" said Tom. "It's okay. He's just making noise. And I don't hear him."

Gristy turned to Tom with a wide grin. "Son," he said. "You're getting more like your Pa every day."

"Thanks," said Tom.

Late that night, lying in his blanket, Tom stared into the dying fire. He couldn't sleep. He thought about Kate and how pretty she looked when she smiled. He knew so little about her. He wanted to know how long she had been out West, and if she liked living in Claytonville. And there was plenty he wanted to tell her, too.

"Tom?" It was Gristy, speaking low.

Tom turned to him. "So you're awake, too," he said.

Gristy nodded. He said, "You know what you said today when Yuba Jack was talking? It was good to hear you say that. Really good."

Tom said, "He was just letting off hot air."

Gristy said, "Not long ago, I think you would have agreed with him."

Tom stared into the night. "You're right," he said. "When Sitlow got Yuba Jack and those other men to go after Pa, I couldn't believe it. I mean, Sitlow lived in the cabin with us. He seemed like a friend."

"But he didn't turn out that way," said Gristy.

Tom shook his head. "When Pa was killed, everyone seemed like Sitlow to me. I forgot about people like you and Dodson."

"You've got to find people you can trust," said Gristy. "Or you'll be lonely all your life."

They were silent for a moment. Then Tom said, "Gristy, what do you think about coming back and living at the cabin? We could start a cattle ranch, like you and Pa were planning to do."

Gristy grinned. "Sounds a lot better than breaking my back digging for gold. I think it would suit me just fine. Now, let's get some shut-eye."

CHAPTER

8

It was late the next afternoon when Tom, Gristy, and Dodson returned to the cabin. They planned to stay there for one night and then take Yuba Jack to Claytonville.

The cabin seemed empty and silent to Tom. It was going to be hard, he thought, being here without Pa. At least Gristy would be here with him.

Gristy stood in the middle of the cabin and yawned. "I could sleep for a week," he said.

Dodson turned to Tom and Gristy. "I'll tell you the truth," he said. I'm getting worried about leaving my claim for so long. Not that it's worth much. But I don't want some claim jumper digging my gold for free."

Gristy looked at Tom. Tom nodded. "You go on ahead, Dodson," said Gristy. "We can handle Yuba Jack the rest of the way to Claytonville."

Dodson said, "I don't want to be running out on you."

"You're not," said Tom. "Don't worry about it."

"All right, then," said Dodson. "I'll say so long for now. I hope to see you both some time again. You're good men to know."

"Same here," said Tom. "Thanks for all your help."

"Good luck to you, Dodson," said Gristy.

The three men shook hands. Then Dodson rode away.

Tom checked the ropes tied around Yuba Jack's hands. "They're awful tight," he complained.

"They're not tight enough to hurt," said Tom. "And you can shut up for a while, so we can get some sleep."

Tom and Gristy rolled out their blankets on the floor. Tom was asleep almost as soon as he shut his eyes.

"Wake up, Tom!" Gristy was shaking him.

Tom opened his eyes. The cabin door was open, and bright light was coming in. "It must be almost noon," he thought with surprise. He had slept all night and into the next day.

"There are riders coming," said Gristy, looking out the door. "Looks like about four or so."

Tom jumped up and grabbed his gun. He looked over at Yuba Jack, tied up in the corner of the cabin. The man was silent, but his eyes were bright. Tom knew he was hoping the riders were friends of his.

Gristy and Tom waited at the cabin door, their guns ready. The riders came close.

Gristy said: "That fellow on the black horse—isn't that Jim McBain?"

Tom smiled, "I think you're right."

"And that's Henry Waybur with him," said Gristy. He and Tom put their guns away.

The riders got off their horses. There were Jim McBain, Henry Waybur, and two other miners, Grant and Bullard.

"Dodson told us you're bringing in Yuba Jack," said McBain. The men went inside to take a look at the prisoner.

"That's him all right," said Waybur. "No mistaking that nose of his."

"People say he's the one who led the stage robbery back in the spring," said Bullard.

"They may just be right," said Gristy.

"But we didn't ride all the way up here just to have a look at Yuba Jack," said McBain. He looked at Waybur, who grinned at Gristy.

"There's a lot of people living around the south fork now," said Waybur. "And more are coming every day. The county's growing pretty fast. I'll get right to the point, Bill Gristy. This county needs a sheriff. And we can't think of a better man than you for the job."

Gristy just stood there, looking surprised.

Grant said, "You've made a name for yourself, the way you caught Yuba Jack and his men."

"Kept a fight from happening in my saloon, too," said Waybur.

Gristy said, "Well, men, being sheriff is a pretty big job. I'm going to have to think about this and let you know. Right now Tom and I have to take Yuba Jack into Claytonville.

The men walked back to their horses.

"You think about it, Gristy," said Waybur. "Why don't you stop on your way back from Claytonville and let us know?"

"I will," said Gristy.

"We hope your answer's yes, Gristy," said McBain.

Tom and Gristy watched the men ride away. "I think you should do it," said Tom.

"I don't want to run out on you, kid," said Gristy.

Tom said, "Don't worry about me. I can find a couple of good men to give me a hand. Dodson was telling me he was fed up with digging for gold. He said he wanted to work on a ranch. I was thinking about offering him a job."

"He's a good man, no doubt about it," said Gristy.

"Sheriff Gristy," said Tom slowly. "Sounds pretty good to me."

"Sounds kind of strange," said Gristy. But his voice was proud.

CHAPTER

9

Tom tied Timber to a post. Gristy had gone to look for the sheriff, leaving Tom with Yuba Jack. Tom looked down the street at the open door of Callahan's, wondering if Kate were inside. As soon as they were finished with Yuba Jack, Tom wanted to see her.

A fat man with a dusty black hat was walking along the wooden sidewalk. "Who you got there, all tied up?" said the man. He pointed to Yuba Jack, who was sitting on the back of Timber.

"His name's Yuba Jack," said Tom.

"Hey, didn't he kill somebody?" said the fat man. "Hey, fellows!" he yelled. "They got Yuba Jack out here!"

A few doors down, two men looked out

of a doorway. One of them yelled, "Yuba Jack?"

Then Tom saw a young woman hurrying out of Callahan's door. It was Kate!

She came up to him, almost running. Her smile was beautiful. "I heard about you going after Yuba Jack," she said. "I'm glad you're all right." her smile disappeared. "I heard about your father, too. I'm sorry. . . ." She broke off. The voices behind her were suddenly loud.

"He ought to be hanged!" the fat man was shouting to his friends.

Three young men were walking up the street. "Who ought to be hanged?" said one of them. He was a young man, but he had a hard face.

"This here Yuba Jack, that's who!" said the fat man.

"Yuba Jack! That's the man who robbed the stage!" said a woman. Tom looked around. Several people were crowding around them.

"Nobody's proved that," said Kate. But the woman didn't even look at her.

"My sister's boy was shot in that holdup!" said another man. "Shot right in the leg."

The young man with the hard face said, "Hanging's the best thing for the likes of Yuba Jack. Let's round up some fellows from the saloon and get ourselves some rope."

Several men joined him, and they hurried up the street. The fat man and a few other people stayed behind. The fat man grinned up at Yuba Jack, who only gave the man a cold stare.

Tom looked at Kate. She came up close to him. "Will your horse be led into a store?" she said in a low voice.

Tom nodded, though he wasn't sure. Kate stepped up to the post, and turned her back to the other people. Quickly, she untied Timber's reins.

"Hey! What do you think you're doing?" said a man.

Tom drew his gun. "Everybody stay put," he said.

Kate led Timber along the wooden sidewalk. Yuba Jack sat silently, his eyes darting like those of a trapped animal. Tom walked behind them, his gun pointed at the group of people.

Kate reached the door of Callahan's. "Duck your head," she said to Yuba Jack.

She pulled on the reins and led Timber inside. "Come in!" she called to Tom.

Tom ran inside. Kate swung the door shut and locked it. There was shouting outside.

"How far away is the sheriff?" said Tom.

"He's clear across town," said Kate.

They could hear loud footsteps on the sidewalk. "He's in here!" someone yelled. "Over here, fellows!"

There were more loud footsteps. "Kate Callahan's got him in there! Her and some young fellow!" It was the fat man's voice.

Someone pounded on the door. "Miss Callahan, you open up!"

"I'll open the door for the sheriff and no one else!" Kate said.

"Never you mind the sheriff. We know what's best for Yuba Jack!"

Kate didn't answer. There was silence for a moment. Then the door shook with a heavy blow, and then another, and another.

"They're kicking the door down," said Kate. Her face was white.

Tom pulled his gun. He took Kate's hand and led her away from the door.

The pounding went on. Tom wondered how long the door would hold.

Then a gun went off. "You men get away from that door!" a voice shouted.

"It's Sheriff Bell," said Kate.

"Move aside," said the sheriff. His voice sounded close now. They could hear him speaking to the crowd. "There's two good reasons for not hanging Yuba Jack," he said. "One is he might have robbed the stage last spring. If he did, maybe we can get him to tell us who was with him, and where we can find them. The second reason is we don't hang people unless they've had a fair trial and been found guilty. Not in this town."

He knocked on the door. "Miss Callahan? This is Sheriff Bell, here. I'd like you to open the door now."

Kate opened the door and looked out. It seemed as if the whole town were standing outside the store.

Sheriff Bell turned to the crowd once more. "Now we're leading Yuba Jack out of here, and we're walking him down to the jail. And don't anybody get ideas about taking a potshot at him. Unless you want to wind up in jail, too." He turned to Kate. "Miss Callahan, you're a brave young woman," the sheriff said.

"Son," he said to Tom, "I understand this is your horse. Want to lead him on out, now?"

Tom led Timber outside. Gristy was standing there, before the door. He grinned at Tom. "Good work, son," he said.

Tom grinned back.

"I'm coming with you," said Kate. Quickly, she stepped up next to Tom. People stood aside for them to pass, and they walked out into the bright afternoon. Tom looked over at Kate. She held her head up proudly as she walked. "Maybe," Tom thought to himself, "I've seen the last of that bad luck for a while."

The Last Cowboy

Leo P. Kelley

1

As the bright sun burned hot in the sky above him, Bart Kendrick bent over and began to dig another hole.

Sweat ran down his face as he worked. The shovel in his hands felt heavy and his whole body felt stiff. But he kept at it, glad that he had a job. It had been a long time since his last one.

Soon the hole was deep enough. Kendrick placed a wooden post in it and filled the hole with dirt. Then he fastened barbed wire to the post. Three hours later, he had finished a barbed wire fence that ran for almost a mile.

Kendrick thumbed his hat back on his head and wiped the sweat from his face. As he did so, he heard a train whistle in the distance. The sound made him think of the past and the way he had once lived. He had been a real cowboy then, driving cattle north through Texas and the Indian country to the railroads in Kansas. At the time there had been only a few railroads. But now they were everywhere.

Cattle ranchers didn't have to go far to ship their cattle to market on a railroad. But twenty years ago, in the 1870s, it was a different story. In those days, cowboys like Bart Kendrick were needed by the Texas cattle ranchers. "But today," thought Kendrick, "we're not as important as we used to be. The days of the long cattle drives are gone forever. These days, there's hardly a place in the world for someone who knows only cowboying and not much else."

Kendrick looked at the length of fence he had built. The sight of it made him sad. It also made him angry. Barbed wire fencing was a sign of the end of the open range. Before the barbed wire had come, cattle grazed freely anywhere there was good grass and water. Nobody owned the range. It was there for everyone to use.

Then came the barbed wire. Fences went up, closing off the open range. The barbed wire and the coming of the railroads had brought an end to Bart Kendrick's way of life. He had been a cowboy ever since he was 17 years old. As time went by, he learned all there was to know about cowboying. By the time he was 21, he had become a top hand. Now, 20 years later, he was a man struggling to find steady work.

"What are you up to, Bart? Having a daydream?"

Kendrick turned around to face the man who had just spoken to him. "No, Lem, I'm not having a daydream. I was just lost in thought, I guess."

"You were thinking about the wire, weren't you? About what it means."

When Kendrick nodded, Lem said, "It's here to stay, you know. It's not going to go away. Not ever."

"I know that, Lem. I guess a man just has to try to get used to the way the world changes."

"I reckon he does, Kendrick. Only trouble is, it seems to me that the changes have been coming too many and too fast of late."

"You miss hunting wild horses, do you, Lem?"

"I do, and that's a true fact. When I was out on the range catching wild horses to break, the world was one real fine place to be. I used to give thanks every day that I was getting to do just what I wanted to do in life."

Kendrick nodded, knowing just what Lem meant.

"There's hardly a wild horse to be found anywhere in Texas these days," Lem went on. "I went north some months ago to the Indian country. But there weren't any to be found there, either. Then I went west and didn't have any better luck there."

"So you ended up stringing fence like me," Kendrick said in a low voice.

"What kind of a job is this?" Lem asked. "Now, I ask you, Kendrick, what kind of a job is this for men like us?"

"Well, I will say this for it, Lem. It puts money in a man's pocket. It keeps him from going hungry."

"You're right on that score, I reckon." Lem was quiet for a minute. Then he asked, "Do you know what we're doing?" Without waiting for an answer, he said, "We're helping to kill what men like us love. I'm talking about the open range. But I'm also talking about more than that.

It's not just a matter of open range. It's also a matter of—"

"Freedom."

Lem pointed a finger at Kendrick and said, "You've just gone and hit the nail right on the head. This fence is what's putting an end to more than just the open range. It's also putting an end to us—to men like you and me, Bart."

"But there's not much, so far as I can see, either one of us can do about it, Lem. I guess all we can do is put up with what's happening."

"And hope it doesn't do us in before it's through."

Kendrick nodded again.

Three days later, Kendrick finished stringing the last of the barbed wire fence for the rancher who had hired him and Lem Peters. He picked up his shovel and other tools and headed for the ranch house. When he reached it, he knocked on the door and waited. After a minute went by, the door was opened by the owner of the ranch.

"I just stopped by to tell you that the fence is all finished, Mr. Bowen."

"Very good, Kendrick," Bowen said. He took some money from his pocket, counted out some bills, and handed them to Kendrick.

Kendrick stared down at the money, but he didn't take it. Instead, he looked up at Bowen and asked, "What's this all about?"

"I'm paying you for the work you did."

"You mean to say you haven't got anything else for me to do?"

Bowen shook his head. "My sons and I can handle everything around here. I just needed a couple of extra men to put up that fence for me."

Kendrick took the money from Bowen and said, "Well, I reckon I'll just head on over to the bunkhouse then. I'll get my gear together and move on out. I thank you for the work, Mr. Bowen. I'm just sorry it couldn't have lasted a little while longer."

"Good luck to you, Kendrick," Bowen called out as Kendrick turned and walked away slowly.

Kendrick found Lem Peters inside the bunkhouse. "Bowen let you go, too?" he asked the other man.

"He did." Lem went on packing his gear.

"Where are you headed now?" Kendrick asked.

"I don't rightly know," Lem answered.

"One place is as good as another, I guess. What about you?"

"I thought maybe I'd head up north."

"How come? Is there work up there?"

"To tell you the truth, I don't know."

"Then why are you planning on heading north?"

"Well, I reckon it will be a bit cooler there than here, what with summer coming on," Kendrick said, grinning.

"I think I'll stay around in these parts for a while," Lem said. "The heat has never bothered me none," he added with a smile.

Then the two men shook hands and Lem left the bunkhouse. Kendrick packed his gear and, ten minutes later, he was also gone. When he got to the barn, he found that both Lem and Lem's horse were gone. He got his horse ready to ride and then swung into the saddle and rode out of the barn. It wasn't long before the Bowen ranch was out of sight behind him. Out of sight, too, was the hated barbed wire fence.

The sun began to drop down in the sky. No wind blew. Kendrick rode on, heading north, the land flat and empty all around him.

It was almost dark that evening when he spotted the smoke rising from a campfire up ahead of him. He rode toward it. When he could see the young man sitting beside the fire, he called out, "Hello, there!"

The man stood up and waved to Kendrick, who then rode up to the campfire.

"Good evening, sir," said the young man. "You are welcome to share my food if you like."

"That's real neighborly of you," Kendrick said and swung down from the saddle.

2

"I hope you like bread and rice," the young man said. He put some of each on a plate and handed the plate to Kendrick.

Taking it from him, Kendrick said, "That will be fine. You know the saying—'beggars can't be choosers.' " Both men sat down by the glowing fire.

"Oh, so that is it. You are a beggar, then."

Kendrick ate some bread before saying, "No, I'm no beggar."

"But you just said—"

"Beggars can't be choosers—that's just something people say. It means if a person gives you something you need, you take it and be glad to get it. Never mind that it may not be just what you want at the time."

"Oh, I think I see now. The English is hard to learn. And sometimes here in the West people have strange ways of saying things."

As he ate, Kendrick kept his eyes on the young man sitting across from him. The man had black eyes. His hair was just as black, and it covered his ears and the back of his neck. His skin was dark and Kendrick wondered if he were a Mexican.

"My name," said the young man, "it is Alonso Franco."

"I'm Bart Kendrick. Are you from Mexico?" Bart asked as he finished the last of the food on his plate.

"No, sir, I am not. I am a Basque. I come from the Pyrenees Mountains in Spain. I have been almost two years in this country."

"What are you doing here, Alonso?"

"I herd my sheep."

"You herd sheep?" Kendrick's voice sounded sharp.

"Yes, sir, it is so. My sheep, they are in among those trees behind us. My sheepdog, King, he guards them for me."

Kendrick put down his empty plate. "I'm a cattleman myself."

"I know what you are not," Alonso said. "You are not a beggar. Now I also know what you are. You are a cowboy. It is so?"

Kendrick had been about to leave. But Alonso's smile made him forget how much he hated sheep. He stayed where he was and nodded. "Yes," he said, "I'm a cowboy. Or I was one, once upon a time."

"You mean you are not a cowboy now? Or is it that I do not understand?"

I'll explain to you what I mean. I used to be a cowboy. But these days, not many people need a man like me. There's not much use for what I know and can do. I know how to work with cattle and horses and how to stay safe and sound out here on the land. People don't much need to know that kind of thing anymore. Now they live in towns and cities, most of them."

"I would not like to live the life of the people in towns and cities," Alonso said, staring into the fire. "It is too fast there. People, they do not talk to each other. They always run, run, run. Run here. Run there. They have no time to live."

Kendrick looked at Alonso. "But you—you do have time to live, is that it?"

"Oh, yes," Alonso said with a cheerful smile. "Out here there is plenty of time to live. To see the sky. To sit in the sun."

"And the rain, what about that?"

Alonso lost his smile. "Yes, the rain. There is time to sit in it, too, and that is not so nice."

"I know what you mean. I've had to sit through many storms—both rain and snow."

"We are then—how you say it—two men the same kind."

"No, I wouldn't say we're two of a kind. Cowboys who herd cattle are a lot different from men who herd sheep."

"You are still a cowboy, then?"

"To tell you the truth, Alonso, I just don't know what I am. I haven't worked with cattle in a long time. The last job I had was building a barbed wire fence. If I am still a cowboy, I reckon I might be, in a way, the *last* cowboy."

"Do all cowboys wear guns?"

Kendrick looked down at the gun that he wore on his right hip. "No, not all cowboys wear guns. But this cowboy does."

"Why?"

"To protect myself."

"From what?"

"Alonso, you sure do ask an awful lot of questions. I wear this gun to protect myself from wild animals—or wild men."

"Have you ever shot a man?"

Kendrick nodded.

"Killed a man?"

Kendrick nodded again. "It's not something I'm proud of. But it had to be done. It was either that, or die myself. And I guess I'm just too mean a man to die." Kendrick tried a smile that didn't work. "But enough talk about me. Tell me about yourself."

"There is not much to tell," Alonso said. "Not much that would be of interest to a cowboy."

"How did you happen to get into the business of herding sheep?"

"Well, it was my job back home in Spain. For three years I work for a man who owned many sheep. Then I met a man back East—another Basque. He tells me that many Basques like us come out here to the West. It is a good place to herd sheep, he says. He is right."

"So you like the life of a sheepherder?" Kendrick asked.

Alonso shrugged his shoulders. "It is a lonely life. A man who herds sheep has only his dog and his sheep for company. Sometimes I do not see another man for months at a time. But I do it still."

"Why?"

"Because one day I will own a big sheep ranch. I will have thousands of sheep on my ranch. I will be a rich man. Already I have 104 sheep."

"Where did you get them?"

"I work for more than one year for a good man. His name is Don Antonio Lucero. He has a big sheep ranch east of here. I ask Don Lucero to pay me for my work with sheep instead of with money. And this he does. Last month I leave Don Lucero and—how you say it—I go out on my own."

"How long do you reckon it will take you to become a rich man?"

"Oh, a long time. But I do not worry about that. I will work hard. I will sell the fleece from my sheep. When I have enough sheep, I will sell some of them for meat. Oh, yes, it will be a long time before I am a rich man. But the time will come. That is the most important thing, is it not?"

"You're right. That's the most important thing."

"Would you like to see my sheep?"

Kendrick was about to say no. But when he saw the proud look on Alonso's face, he didn't have the heart to turn him down. "Sure," he said. "I'd like to have a look at your sheep."

Alonso jumped to his feet and started for the trees where the sheep were. Kendrick joined him.

"You will meet my sheepdog, King," Alonso said. "King is the best dog a man could want. He works very hard—like me. Together we make a good team, King and me."

Kendrick and Alonso had almost reached the trees when they heard a dog begin to bark.

"That is King," Alonso said. "Something must be wrong with the flock. King never barks unless there is something wrong." He began to run toward the sound of the barking dog.

Kendrick hurried after him. When he reached the flock, he saw five wolves attacking Alonso's sheep. He watched as the sheep ran in every direction to escape from the wolves. One of the wolves caught and brought down one of the sheep. Alonso began shouting at the top of his voice.

"That boy is a fool," Kendrick thought, as he saw Alonso run toward the attacking wolf. "Does he think he's going to tear that wolf apart with nothing but his two hands? More likely that wolf will tear him apart."

Kendrick drew his gun.

CHAPTER

3

As Alonso ran toward the wolf, he waved his arms in front of him to chase it away. The wolf turned from the sheep it had just killed to face Alonso. Its lips drew back over its bloody white fangs. It made a noise deep in its throat and got ready to spring.

Because he was running so fast, Alonso was not able to stop. The wolf leaped into the air, mouth wide open and claws ready for another kill.

But before the wolf could reach Alonso, Kendrick fired his gun. The animal let out an awful howl before falling to the ground at Alonso's feet. Alonso stood stiffly, staring down at the dead wolf as Kendrick ran toward him, shouting his name.

"Those wolves don't care where they get their meat!" Kendrick shouted at him. "From the sheep or from you. *Take cover!*"

Alonso ran behind a large pile of rocks.

Kendrick fired a second time and another wolf went down. All around Kendrick, sheep ran in every direction as they tried to escape from the wolves. King was barking loudly as he tried to drive the wolves away. One of the sheep ran into Kendrick and almost knocked him down. The blow spoiled the shot he fired. It caused him to completely miss the wolf he was shooting at.

The animal had its sharp teeth in the neck of one of the sheep. It shook the sheep, trying to kill it. Then, the wolf turned, so that it had the sheep between itself and Kendrick. Kendrick knew that if he fired at the wolf he would hit the sheep instead.

"You think you're so smart, do you?" Kendrick said silently to the wolf. "Well, I'm smarter." He quickly ran to one side, raised the gun in his hand, and fired. He hit the wolf, and it let go of the sheep. The wolf snapped at the spot on its body where Kendrick's bullet had hit. It began to run in a circle, falling down and then getting back up again.

"You might as well lie down," Kendrick silently told the wolf. "Because you're dead, and I know it even if you don't." As if it had heard Kendrick's thoughts, the wolf fell to the ground and lay still.

"*Look out!*"

Kendrick heard Alonso's shout and quickly turned around. One of the two remaining wolves was about to spring on him. He knew the wolf would go for his throat. He pulled back the hammer of his gun, and as the wolf leaped at him he dropped down on one knee. He aimed, squeezed the trigger, and fired at the wolf, hitting it in the heart.

Kendrick stood up again and turned to find Alonso throwing rocks at the one remaining wolf. A few of the rocks hit the animal, but many of them missed. Just as Kendrick was about to shoot the wolf, Alonso hit it on the head with a big rock. The wolf turned tail and ran.

Alonso came out from behind the pile of rocks with a smile on his face. "I got one , " he said. "But you got four."

"That's true—in a manner of speaking," Kendrick told him. "But your wolf is still alive. It might come back one day—with some friends. Do you remember that I said I carry a gun to protect myself from wild animals?"

"Yes, I do. And also you said you carry it to protect you from wild men."

"Right. Well, Alonso, I think it would be a good idea if you got yourself a gun. You should get one the first chance you get."

"I think you are right. I must get myself a good gun. As you said, that wolf that ran away might come back with some other wolves." Alonso stopped speaking for a moment, and then he held out his hand. As Kendrick shook it, Alonso said, "Thank you, Bart Kendrick, for helping me save my flock."

"We didn't save all of it," Kendrick said. He pointed to the dead sheep that lay on the ground nearby.

"I am very sorry to lose that sheep," Alonso said. "But if it had not been for you, I might have lost all of them."

"I'm glad I could be of some help to you."

"There is another way you could be of help to me, Bart."

"Oh? Which way is that?"

"You could come to work for me."

Kendrick was taken completely by surprise. "I don't believe it," he thought. "Here is this kid asking me, a grown man, to come to work for him. And on top of that he's a sheepherder. Someone should tell him that cowboys don't care much for working with sheep."

"What do you say, Bart?"

Before Kendrick could answer, King ran up and jumped on him. He bent down and patted the dog's head.

"King likes you, too," Alonso said. "With the three of us guarding the flock, I am sure the sheep would come to no harm."

Kendrick stopped petting King. He looked at Alonso and said, "I hate to turn you down. But I just can't take a job herding sheep."

"You have some place you must go to?"

"No, it's not that," Kendrick answered.

"You do not want to work?"

"Sure, I want to work. In fact, I need a job. But—"

"Then it is, how you say, all settled. You have a job. You will work for me."

"No, I won't." Kendrick knew he would have to tell Alonso the truth. "It's got nothing to do with you as a person, Alonso. You're a nice enough kid. And

King's a fine dog. It's that I just can't work with sheep."

Alonso's face fell.

"But I will help you round up your flock before I move on," Kendrick said.

"You do not have to do that. King and I can do it."

"I want to," Kendrick said. Then with King at his heels, he moved deeper into the trees to hunt for the sheep that the wolves had driven off. He looked back over his shoulder. When he saw that Alonso wasn't following him, he waved the young man on.

Alonso then followed, and with King's help they began to round up the remaining sheep. Everything went smoothly until they came to a stream. There they found three sheep standing still in the water.

Alonso went into the water and tried to pull one of the sheep out. King stood on dry land barking, but the sheep did not move.

"Hold on a minute," Kendrick called out and then went to his horse. When he returned, he was carrying a long rope that had been hanging from his saddle horn. He walked into the water and tied one end of the rope around the neck of the sheep. Then he walked back to the land and began to pull on the rope.

Alonso stepped out of the stream and also took hold of Kendrick's rope.

"Their fleece is wet and heavy," Kendrick said to Alonso. "That's why they can't move on their own." Alonso nodded in agreement. "Pull as hard as you can, boy," Kendrick said.

Minutes later they had the first sheep out of the stream and standing on dry ground. But it took them 15 more minutes to get the other two sheep out of the stream. They had no sooner done so than Kendrick noticed dust rising in the distance.

Alonso turned, and when he also saw the dust he asked Kendrick what it was.

"Two riders coming this way," Kendrick answered. "Their horses are kicking up that dust."

"Good," said Alonso. "We will have some company."

"Maybe it's not so good," Kendrick said in a low voice.

"What do you mean by that, Bart?"

"Sometimes strangers riding up on a camp without as much as a shout can mean trouble."

"Trouble? What kind of trouble?"

"There are many kinds of trouble," Kendrick said. "But we won't judge anybody until we see what they want," Kendrick said.

They watched as the two riders kept coming closer. Finally they came to a stop. Silently they sat in their saddles looking down at Kendrick and Alonso.

CHAPTER

4

"Well, if it isn't my old partner!" said one of the riders as he stared down at Kendrick. "Where have you been keeping yourself, Kendrick?"

"Here and there, McDade," Kendrick answered. "What about you? How has the world been treating you?"

"Oh, I'm doing fine these days. Got me a job with a man named Drew. He owns a cattle ranch over on the other side of that hill back there." McDade pointed to a hill in the distance behind him.

"It looks like you know this man, McDade," said the other rider.

"That's right, Quinn," McDade said. "I know him real well. We used to be partners a long time ago up in Kansas. His name is Bart Kendrick." To Kendrick, McDade said, "Those were some good times for the two of us, weren't they, Kendrick?"

"They were that, McDade."

"So what happened?"

"What do you mean what happened?"

"I mean it's clear as day that you've gone and fallen on hard times."

"Now what makes you think a thing like that, McDade?"

"Sheep," McDade answered, pointing to the flock in the distance. "You sure must have fallen on hard times to be messing around with a flock of stinking sheep— and this kid here."

"I am not a kid," Alonso said. "I—"

"Shut your mouth," Quinn barked. "You speak when you're spoken to. And nobody spoke a word to you yet."

"You can't tell me what to do," Alonso shouted at Quinn.

Quinn's hand dropped to the gun he wore on his hip.

But before Quinn could draw his gun, Kendrick's gun was in his hand and aimed right at him. "I'd leave that gun right where it is if I were you," Kendrick told Quinn in a cold voice.

Their eyes met. A moment later, Quinn dropped his eyes. Kendrick kept his gun in his hand as he turned to McDade. "How come you and your gun-happy friend took it upon yourselves to pay us a visit?"

"Those sheep are the reason," McDade answered. "Like I told you, Mr. Drew raises cattle. And he don't like sheep any better than me and Quinn do. He don't what them on his range because he needs all the grass and water around here for his cattle. So when he found out those sheep were here, he sent Quinn and me over with a message."

"What message?" Alonso asked.

"Mr. Drew wants you and all your stinking sheep off his range," McDade said.

"This is open range," Alonso said. "It's land owned by the government. Anyone can use it."

McDade sadly shook his head. "Quinn, this kid has no more sense than a snake. Tell him."

Quinn said, "Mr. Drew got all the men who work for him to take out claims on the range around his ranch. So now all this range as far—even farther—than you can see belongs to him."

"Wait a minute," Kendrick said. "A man can keep a claim only if he works the land and builds a house on it. That's the law."

"Well, who is to say that all of us don't mean to do that very thing on each one of our claims?" Quinn snapped back.

"I don't believe any of you mean to build a house on your claim or farm the land," Kendrick said flatly.

"What you believe or don't believe don't mean a thing to us," Quinn told Kendrick.

"There's only one fact that matters," McDade said. "Mr. Drew now controls all the range around here because of the claims we took out. He's got the right to order anyone he wants off his land. And he's ordering you and your partner off, Kendrick."

"If you're not gone in 48 hours . . . ," Quinn added, but he didn't finish his sentence. His right hand patted his gun.

"Oh, I almost forgot," McDade said. "Mr. Drew told us to tell you that he has set up a boundary down there." McDade turned around in his saddle and pointed. "Mr. Drew's boundary runs due east and west just 40 yards from here."

"And if either one of you so much as sets a single foot over Mr. Drew's boundary, you just might wind up dead."

"But that means my sheep cannot get to water," Alonso said. "The boundary you speak of cuts them off from the stream. If they cannot get to water, they will all die."

"Then you better take your sheep someplace where they can get to water," Quinn said and then laughed.

"All this doesn't have to be a problem for you, Kendrick," McDade said. "I don't know how you got yourself into such a sorry mess as to end up here herding sheep with this kid. But I reckon Mr. Drew would be glad to take on a man like you who knows how to handle cattle. Why don't you ride back with us to the ranch? I'll be glad to put in a good word for you with Mr. Drew."

Kendrick shook his head. "No, thanks, McDade. I like it fine right where I am."

"Suit yourself," McDade snapped. "But remember. Don't cross the boundary."

"And be long gone from here by the day after tomorrow," Quinn added.

Kendrick watched as both men turned their horses and rode back the way they had come.

"I wonder," Alonso said.

"You wonder what?" Kendrick asked as he watched McDade and Quinn ride off.

"I wonder why it is that you did not go with your friend to the ranch of Mr. Drew. There you probably would find work like McDade said. Work you like to do. Work with cattle, not sheep."

Kendrick said, "I don't like it when men like Drew send men like McDade and Quinn to push other people around. I don't reckon I'd last long working for Drew. Sooner or later we would be sure to have ourselves a run-in. And then I'd have to be moving on."

"But you will be moving on now anyway, yes?"

A part of Kendrick wanted to say "Yes," he would indeed be moving on. But, to his great surprise, another part of him wanted to stay with Alonso and the flock.

Alonso asked his question a second time.

"No, Alonso," Kendrick answered. "I don't think I'll be moving on. Not yet, anyway."

"You mean—"

"I mean I plan on taking that job you offered me a little while ago. If the pay is good, that is." He grinned.

Alonso gave him a big smile. But a moment later, his smile went away. "I think I understand, Bart. You have decided to stay to protect me from McDade and Quinn. Well, I can take care of myself— and my sheep. I don't need your help."

"You've got it all wrong, boy," Kendrick lied. "That's not what made me decide to stay on here," he said. "I just want to settle down for a spell, quit moving around all the time. I reckon this is as good a place as any to do that."

Alonso stared hard at Kendrick and said nothing for a moment. Then his smile returned and he said, "Then we are—how you say it—partners?"

"You got it, kid. That's what we are from now on. Partners."

"Good. I am glad. Now , there is work to do."

"Where are you going?"

"To take my sheep to the stream so that they may drink."

"The boundary—"

"My sheep must have water," Alonso said. "But do not worry, Bart. We will move the flock from here the day after tomorrow."

"Then you don't mean to stay here and stand your ground against Drew and his men?"

"You do not understand, Bart. I planned to move the flock by then, anyway. We will take them to Don Lucero's ranch. There they will have their fleece shorn. Don Lucero pays some men to do that work every spring. Then, when the sheep are all shorn, we will come back here."

As Alonso and King herded the sheep down the stream, Kendrick shook his head. "It's a good thing I decided to throw in with the boy," he thought. "Maybe I can keep him from getting himself killed."

CHAPTER

5

Early the next morning, Kendrick left Alonso and rode alone into a nearby town. He went first to a general store where he asked the man there to show him some guns. After carefully looking over each of the guns, Kendrick bought the one he liked best.

"I'll need some shells for this gun," he told the man in the store. Kendrick then paid the man for both the gun and shells and he left the store.

Outside, Kendrick crossed the dirt street and went into the livery stables. He asked the man he found there to show him what horses he had for sale.

The man brought out two horses, one black and one dark brown. Kendrick looked both of them over very carefully.

He checked their teeth first, then their eyes. He looked at the shoes on their feet to make sure they weren't loose. Then he stepped back and slowly walked around the black horse, running his hand along its body. A moment later he did the same with the dark brown horse.

"They're both good horses," the livery man said. "I can let you have the black one for twenty dollars and the brown one for fifteen."

Kendrick took another close look at the black. "It's got a nice big chest," he thought. "That means it's got good wind. Judging by its teeth, the brown one is about three or four years older than the black." Kendrick made up his mind to buy the black.

Turning to the man at his side, he said, "I'll give you fifteen dollars for the black."

The man shook his head. "I don't give good horses like that big black away."

"I'm not asking you to give him away. I said I'd pay you fifteen dollars for him."

"That's about the same as giving him away," the man said. "As it is, I'm letting him go for less than he's really worth. Why, I could get twenty-five dollars for him any day of the week."

"Sixteen dollars," Kendrick said.

"Nineteen," the man said.

Five minutes later, Kendrick and the man settled on a price of eighteen dollars and fifty cents for the black. Kendrick paid the man, and then also bought a secondhand saddle and other gear to put on the horse. Then he put the gear on the big black and led the animal out of the livery to where he had left his own horse.

Kendrick climbed onto the saddle of his horse. Then leading the black he had just bought, he headed back to where he had left Alonso. By the time he reached the spot, it was almost noon.

When Alonso saw Kendrick coming, he ran to meet him. "What is this?" he asked, pointing to the big black.

"What does it look like? It's a horse," Kendrick said as he swung down from the saddle.

"The black is yours and so is the gear he's got on him." He handed the gun and box of shells he had bought to Alonso. "This gun and these shells are also yours. All in all, you owe me forty-nine dollars and fifty cents."

"What are they for, this gun and that horse?"

"Alonso, you don't strike me as being stupid. But that sure is a stupid question you just asked me. The gun is to help protect you in case of trouble. The horse is to ride."

"But sheepherders, we do not ride horses, Bart. We walk."

"Well, you're one sheepherder who is going to learn how to ride. I'm going to teach you to ride as well as any cowboy ever did. Including the cowboy you're looking at right now."

"You will also teach me how to shoot this?" Alonso held up the gun in two fingers as if he were afraid to touch it.

"That, too. Come on. I think it's about time for school to start. Let's start the lessons with that gun." Kendrick took the gun from Alonso and showed him how to load it.

"Why do you put in only five shells, Bart? There is room for six."

"It's a good idea to leave one space empty for the hammer of the gun to rest on. With an empty space under the hammer, there's no chance that the gun could go off by accident."

"Now, then," Kendrick said, looking around. "We can use that tree over there to shoot at."

"But it is so thin," Alonso said. "I don't think I can hit it."

Kendrick took aim at the tree, fired, and hit it. Then he gave the gun to Alonso and showed him how to hold it.

"It's heavy," Alonso said.

"You'll get used to it. Now, take aim. No, don't look down at the gun. Keep your eye on what you're going to shoot at. In this case, that tree over there. Now sight along the barrel of the gun."

Alonso did, and fired. But his shot went into the ground several feet short of the big tree. "What did I do wrong, Bart?"

"For one thing, you let the gun slip down before you fired. For another, you *pulled* the trigger. Don't pull the trigger. Squeeze it slow and easy like."

Alonso nodded and then raised the gun again.

"Higher," Kendrick said.

Alonso raised the gun higher and closed his left eye.

"Keep both of your eyes wide open," Kendrick ordered him. "You want to be able to see what you're shooting at. Now, remember. *Squeeze* the trigger. Don't pull it like before."

Alonso fired a second time, and this time his shot hit the tree. He smiled at Kendrick and then fired a third shot. This one missed the tree as badly as the first one had.

"It takes a lot of practice to be a good shot," Kendrick told him.

Alonso shot twice more, missing the tree both times. Then he put five more shells in his empty gun. By mid-afternoon he was hitting the tree four out of every five times he fired.

"You're doing fine," Kendrick told him. "Nobody hits what he's aiming at every single time. Now, let's see if I can teach you to ride that big black I got for you."

They went over to where they had tied up the horse. The big black stood very still, its great eyes on Alonso. Looking brave and determined, Alonso placed his gun under his belt, and began to mount the horse.

"No, not like that," Kendrick said as Alonso put his right foot into the right stirrup. "You climb up from the left side."

"Why is that?" Alonso asked as he came around the left side.

"I don't know, to tell you the truth," Kendrick said. "But that's the way it is— for white men, anyway. You take Indians now. They climb aboard a horse from the right side like you were about to do."

When Alonso was seated in the saddle, Kendrick stepped closer to the black. He said to Alonso, "Hold the reins in both hands at first, boy. Until you get the hang of this business. Don't hold them too tight. Your horse won't be able to move his head when he walks or gallops. He needs to be able to do that to move fast and easy. Hold the reins kind of loose. But not so loose that you lose control of the horse. Now, move out nice and slow."

As Alonso moved the black out slowly, Kendrick closely watched him and the horse. "Take it easy, boy. You're as stiff as a board. Sit up straight, but sit in your saddle easy. That's it. That's good!"

Alonso rode the black in a circle. In a few minutes he returned to the place where he had started. Kendrick said, "When you want to turn to the right, pull on the right rein and lean your body a little to the left."

As Alonso followed Kendrick's directions, the black made a smooth turn to the right, tossing its head as it did so.

"That's real good, boy. Are you sure you never rode a horse before?"

Alonso laughed. "The only animal I ever rode—or tried to—was a big dog I had when I was a boy of only five years old." He pulled on the left rein and the black turned sharply but smoothly to the left.

"Let him gallop!" Kendrick called out. "And hold on—but not too tight."

The black galloped away. Then Alonso turned the horse around and rode back toward Kendrick. When he reached his teacher, he pulled on both reins and the horse came to a sudden stop.

"Not like that," Kendrick said.

"What did I do wrong?"

"When you're ready to stop, stand up a little in your stirrups. When you do that, it makes it easy for your horse to get his back legs up and under him. And another thing. Don't let your legs flop up and down when you ride. You do that and you'll have trouble keeping control of your horse. Now, try it again."

For the next hour, Kendrick tried to teach Alonso everything he knew about riding a horse. He was pleased at how quickly and how well Alonso learned everything. "That's enough for today," he then told Alonso.

"I don't want to stop now, not when I'm doing so well."

"Well, you'd better stop, take it from me. As it is, come tomorrow you're going to be stiff and sore just about all over. And tomorrow we'll be herding your sheep to Don Lucero's ranch. We don't want to wait any longer or we'll have McDade and Quinn showing up to run us off."

"I am not afraid of them."

"Maybe you should be. A touch of fear can be good for your health. It can help you stay alive and kicking."

"Are you afraid of McDade and Quinn?"

Kendrick smiled slightly and said, "Not so afraid that I won't be able to fight them if and when the time comes. And I reckon it will come—sooner or later."

6

Kendrick and Alonso rode side by side the next morning as they herded the sheep toward Don Lucero's ranch. King ran between the two sheepherders and the sheep. He barked and snapped at the heels of the sheep to keep them moving.

"This is almost like riding drag on a cattle drive," Kendrick said. "A man is forced to eat some dust in either case."

"Do you have dogs to help you drive cattle?" Alonso asked.

Kendrick shook his head.

"Without dogs to help you, how do you keep the cattle all together?"

"Men ride on either side of the herd to keep them in line," Kendrick explained. "Two men ride at the front of the herd.

They're called point men. The two on either side behind the point men are the swing men. Behind the swing men ride the two flank men, one on each side. Behind the herd come the men riding drag."

"Don't any of the cattle ever try to run away?"

"Sure, some do at times. We just go after them, catch them, and bring them right back to the herd."

"How do you catch them if you have no dogs to chase them for you?"

"Hold up here for a minute. I can show you better than I can tell you." Alonso brought his horse to a stop. Kendrick rode up to the flock and drove a single sheep from it. Then he took the rope that hung from his saddle horn and quickly made it into a lariat. King started to chase the sheep that Kendrick had driven from the flock. But Kendrick had Alonso call the dog back.

Then Kendrick gave a loud yell and sent his horse galloping after the lone sheep. He swung the loop of the lariat in a wide circle above his head. As he came close to the sheep he threw the lariat and it dropped down around the animal's neck.

Then Kendrick stopped his horse, and the sheep was also forced to come to a stop. After turning his horse, Kendrick rode back to the flock, leading the sheep with the lariat still looped around its neck.

"I think I will stay with King," Alonso said. "I could never do what you just did."

"Sure, you could," Kendrick said. He removed his lariat from the sheep and let it return to the flock. "It just takes practice until you get the hang of it. Want to give it a try?"

Alonso nodded. Kendrick showed him how to hold the lariat and then how to throw it. Once again he drove a single sheep from the flock, and watched as Alonso went galloping after it. He laughed when Alonso threw the lariat and it went wide of its mark. He kept watching as Alonso turned his horse and tried again. This time, when Alonso threw the lariat, it landed squarely around the neck of the sheep.

Alonso shook the lariat free and then began to chase the sheep again. He practiced throwing the lariat for almost a half hour. Then the two men rode on until they reached Don Lucero's ranch. Alonso left the flock to graze near the house. Then he got down from his horse, went to the front door, and knocked. It was opened by a short, fat man with dark hair and brown eyes. When he saw Alonso, the man threw his arms around him. He held Alonso out in front of him at arm's length. "It is good to see you again, young man," he said. "You look well."

"I am well, Don Lucero," Alonso said. "I have come with my new partner for the shearing of the sheep. Don Lucero, I would like for you to meet Bart Kendrick."

Don Lucero shaded his eyes from the sun and looked up at Kendrick. "How do you do, señor?" He held up his hand and Kendrick shook it.

I'm glad to meet you, Don Lucero," Kendrick said. "You've got yourself a real nice place here."

"Thank you. It is the result of hard work over many years. You are welcome here, Señor Kendrick."

As Kendrick swung down from the saddle, Don Lucero called to a man who was working nearby. The man walked over and took Kendrick's and Alonso's horses to a barn. "Come inside," Don Lucero said. "You shall have something to eat and drink before the shearing begins this afternoon."

"The shearers are here?" Alonso asked as they entered the house.

"They came early this morning. They were at a ranch 20 miles from here yesterday. There are many sheep to be shorn in this part of the country these days. Those shearers are very busy. If they keep on this way they will all get rich shearing the sheep of ranchers like myself."

Later, the three men sat in the kitchen finishing the lunch the ranch cook had fixed for them. Don Lucero turned to Alonso and asked, "How is your flock? Safe, I hope."

"There was some trouble, Don Lucero," Alonso said.

"Trouble? What kind of trouble? Were you hurt?"

"No," Alonso said. "But one of my sheep was killed."

"What happened?"

Alonso told Don Lucero about the wolves that had attacked the flock. Then he said, "But that is not the worst trouble I had."

"What could be worse than wolves?" Don Lucero asked. And then his eyes suddenly grew wide. "I know. I mean I think I can guess what trouble you have that is worse by far than wolves. You have trouble with cattlemen. It is so?"

"It is so, Don Lucero," Alonso answered. "Two men, they come to where Bart and I were with the flock. These men say we are on land that belongs to someone named Drew. They say we must leave the land or they will make trouble for us."

"So you left. Good." Don Lucero reached out and patted Alonso on the shoulder.

"But I am going back," Alonso said stiffly. "There is good grass there and plenty of water. It is a much better place than any other I have found near here."

"Alonso," Don Lucero said, "that is foolish talk. You must not go back there. Those men you spoke of, they may try to kill you. It has happened before during range wars between cattlemen and sheepherders."

"I have made up my mind," Alonso said.

Don Lucero turned to Kendrick, a look of worry on his face. "Señor Kendrick, this is terrible."

"It could be," Kendrick said. "I've been in range wars in my time—on the cattlemen's side. They're never pretty. Men get hurt. Killed, too, sometimes."

"Am I to understand that you are willing to let Alonso be hurt—or killed?" Don Lucero asked Kendrick.

"No, I'm not," Kendrick answered. "But I think a man has to stand up and fight for what is his. And Alonso seems bent on doing that very thing. It looks like he won't let Drew or his men push him around. In that way, I guess you could say Alonso and me are two of a kind."

"It is a good thing to fight for what you know is right," Don Lucero said slowly. "I have done my share of fighting in my life. But Alonso is like a son to me. I do not want him to come to any harm. I do not want to see either of you come to any harm."

"I will not get hurt," Alonso promised Don Lucero with a smile on his face.

"The young," said Don Lucero, shaking his head. "They all think they will live forever."

"It is not that," Alonso said. "Bart, he teaches me to defend myself. See, Don Lucero, this is my new gun. Bart, he teaches me how to shoot it. He also teaches me how to ride my horse. And how to catch sheep who run from the flock with a lariat! So there is no need for you to worry about me."

To Kendrick, Don Lucero said, "Perhaps you can talk some sense into the head of your foolish partner."

"Don Lucero," Kendrick began. "Alonso may indeed be foolish like you seem to think. On the other hand, you could call him brave. Sometimes there is not a whole lot of difference between the two."

"What of your dream to own your own sheep ranch one day?" Don Lucero asked Alonso. "If you fight against the cattlemen, you may die. What then of your wonderful dream?"

"I will not die," Alonso said softly. "I have too much to live for—my dream for one very beautiful thing."

"Well, then, there is one thing I can do to try to keep you from getting hurt or killed," said Don Lucero. "I will send word to all the other sheep ranchers around here. I will pay a reward of one thousand dollars for the capture and arrest of anyone who causes harm to you or your partner, or to any of your sheep, Alonso."

"Thank you, Don Lucero," Alonso said.

"That's a real good idea, Don Lucero," Kendrick said. "When word of the reward goes out, maybe Drew's men will back off. Then Alonso and I will each be able to stay in one piece."

Don Lucero got to his feet. "Come, Señor Kendrick. I will show you how the men shear the sheep. It is done every spring."

CHAPTER

7

"Take care of yourself, Alonso," Don Lucero said as Alonso and Kendrick got ready to leave the next morning.

"I hope you will get a good price when you sell all the fleece from my sheep," Alonso said.

"You can be sure I will," Don Lucero said. "When I have sold your fleece in town, I will send you the money."

Alonso climbed into his saddle and moved his horse out. Kendrick waved to Don Lucero and began to follow Alonso.

Suddenly, Don Lucero ran up to Kendrick, who drew up on the reins as Alonso rode on ahead.

"Señor Kendrick, I beg you—look after Alonso. Do not let him do anything foolish."

"I'll do my best to look out for him—and for myself, too," Kendrick promised. And then he rode away to catch up with Alonso.

Ahead of them, King helped to herd the sheep. Without their thick fleece, the animals looked much smaller and thinner.

As they rode on together, Kendrick said, "Indians came by here some time back."

"How do you know that?"

"See that little tree over there? It's growing parallel to the ground instead of straight up like it should."

"Yes, I see it. But what—"

"Indians do that. They bend trees to point in the direction they are going. That way other Indians coming along later can find them."

"I never would have noticed that tree," Alonso said. "Even if I had, I wouldn't have known why it is growing the way it is. How did you learn that?"

"Oh, you get to learn a whole lot of things when you've been cowboying as long as I have. You also learn other ways of marking your trail to tell somebody which way you went. One way to do it is to place one rock on top of another and another one beside them to point out the way. Or you can break a branch of a tree so that it points in the direction you went."

Kendrick went on to tell Alonso more about what he called "reading sign." He explained that you could tell if a horse had a rider by how deep its feet dug into the ground. Horses with riders dig deeper into the ground than those without them. He said that there was a good chance a horse belonged to an Indian if it had no shoes on it. And you could tell by the horse's tracks whether or not it was wearing shoes.

You could tell if a rider was making his horse gallop or if he was walking it by looking at the distance between the horse's footprints. You could tell how far ahead of you a rider was if you found the droppings left by the rider's horse. If they were wet, the horse was not far ahead. But if the droppings were dry, they had been there for some time. So you knew that the rider was probably far ahead of you.

"Same thing with a campfire," Kendrick went on. "If the ashes of a dead fire are warm, you know the person who built the fire hasn't been gone long. But if they're cold, you know he's been gone for a while.

"When you're tracking somebody, look for a sign of where he's been. Look for things like a broken branch, earth dug up by his horse, bent grass, broken bushes. If you keep your eyes open, you'll soon be able to read signs easily. Just as if the land and the things on it were telling you all their secrets."

By the time they reached the grazing ground they had left the day before, Kendrick had almost run out of things to tell Alonso. But Alonso had not run out of questions to ask him. They talked on and on, Kendrick teaching and Alonso learning. Finally they had moved the sheep where they wanted, and they left King to stand guard over them.

"I'll build a fire and we can fix something to eat," Alonso said and went looking for wood. When he came back, Kendrick told him not to use the wood he'd gathered.

"Why not?" Alonso wanted to know.

"It's green wood," Kendrick said. "It'll make too much smoke. Green or wet wood makes a lot of smoke. And smoke can tell somebody where you are. Right now we don't want to tell anyone where we are."

"You mean anyone like McDade or Quinn."

"You got it." Kendrick left Alonso, and when he returned he was carrying some old dry wood he had gathered. He went in among some trees and built a fire under them. When Alonso joined him, Kendrick said, "Any smoke this wood gives off will get lost up there in the tree branches. So it's not likely to be seen by anyone."

Later, after they had finished their meal, Kendrick said, "Tonight we'll take turns standing watch."

"You mean in case McDade or Quinn shows up again."

"That's right. I'll take the first watch. I'll wake you up around 2:00 A.M. for your watch."

After they had cleaned up, Kendrick went to the top of a nearby hill to stand the first watch. The night air turned cool. The moon rose, and night birds called in the distance. Kendrick sat with his back up against a tree.

With the bright light of the moon shining down, Kendrick could see the sheep sleeping below the hill. He watched as King walked silently around the flock. He thought that, because of the dog, standing watch might not really be necessary. If somebody were to come near the sheep during the night, King would hear the noise and start to bark. Still, he decided, it's better to be safe than sorry.

Hours later, Kendrick knew that it was time to wake Alonso. He got up and made his way down the hill. King heard him coming and gave a single bark. Then, when the dog saw that it was Kendrick, he stopped barking.

"Good boy," Kendrick said softly and bent down to pet the dog. Then he moved on to the camp where the fire had been allowed to burn itself out. He woke Alonso, who sat up and asked him what time it was.

"It's time for you to stand watch," Kendrick answered. "There are about four hours before dawn. I'll see you back here then."

When Alonso had gone to stand watch, Kendrick lay down on his blanket and covered himself up. He was asleep in minutes.

He was awakened hours later by the sound of Alonso shouting in the distance. His eyes snapped open and he quickly got up. In a moment Alonso came running toward him through the trees.

"What's wrong?" he asked as Alonso reached him.

"It's King," Alonso answered. "It is all my fault."

"What about King?" Kendrick asked.

"King is dead, Bart. When I woke up, I found him lying on the ground with his throat cut."

"When you woke up—"

"I could not help it. I fell asleep," Alonso confessed. "It just happened."

"Well, it never should have happened," Kendrick snapped in anger. "You never should have *let* it happen. When a man has a job to do, he does it—and he does it right. You had a job to do and you didn't do it. Don't you know that whoever cut King's throat could also have cut yours—and then mine, too?"

"I am sorry, Bart."

"Feeling sorry won't bring King back to life."

Alonso hung his head under Kendrick's hard stare and angry words.

"One of us had better get back to the flock," Kendrick said. "If we don't, we might find all the sheep with their throats cut next."

"I will go," Alonso said, running back the way he had come. He had not gone far when he stopped and turned around. "Do you think McDade or Quinn did this?" he asked.

"I reckon one of them did it," Kendrick answered. "Or maybe the pair of them did it. I don't know who else would want to do a thing like that. Get moving, boy, and drive the flock back this way."

Kendrick spent a few minutes building a fire to cook breakfast. Moments later, Alonso once again came running back to their camp.

"Bart!" he cried. "The sheep—some of them are dead and many more are dying!"

8

"The sheep were still asleep when I found King," Alonso explained to Kendrick. "When I got back they were starting to graze. But some of them didn't get up. I took a close look and found they were dead and many more were dying. I don't know what happened to them."

Kendrick and Alonso ran to the spot where the flock was. Then Kendrick said, "We've got to get those that are still alive out of here. Let's do it!"

They moved quickly. In minutes, they had the living sheep far away from those that were dead.

"Bart, what could have killed them?" Alonso asked. "Their throats were not cut. They were not shot. I do not understand what happened to them."

Kendrick went back to where the sheep had been kept for the night. He got down on one knee and studied the ground. When Alonso appeared at his side, he pointed to the ground and said: "Saltpeter."

"Saltpeter? What is saltpeter?"

Kendrick stood up. "Saltpeter is a fertilizer. It harms sheep, but not cattle. A lot of cattlemen have been known to spread it on the ground to kill sheep. They know it won't hurt their cattle if they eat it. So, for them it's safe to use."

"Cattlemen." Alonso said it so softly Kendrick could hardly hear him. "Drew," he said. And then, "McDade and Quinn."

"They might have done it," Kendrick said. "Maybe they saw us come back and decided to try to run us off by killing our sheep. But we don't have any proof that they did."

"This is all my fault," Alonso said. "If only I had not fallen asleep! I might have heard whoever spread the saltpeter and killed King."

"Whoever it was must have caught King asleep," Kendrick said. "Or maybe King barked, but you didn't hear him. We won't ever know for sure."

Alonso began to count the sheep that were either dead or very sick. "Eight are dead and six more are dying," he said when he had finished. "I'm glad they were shorn before they were killed. We will have money from the sale of their fleece, at least."

"You know what all this means, don't you?" Kendrick asked.

Alonso looked at him with a blank stare. "It's a warning, that's what it is," Kendrick said. "It's a way of telling us to get out of here. If we don't get out, I reckon we'll find ourselves facing even more trouble down the line."

"I will move the sheep away from this place," Alonso said.

"You've decided to turn tail and run, have you?"

Alonso shook his head. "No, I have not. I will stay on this range, but far from the saltpeter in this place. But you do not have to stay here with me, Bart," he added. "I will understand if you decide to move on to a place that's safe."

"Are you trying to run me off, boy?"

"No, I did not mean that. But I thought you might want to leave before there is any more trouble."

Kendrick and Alonso stared silently at each other for a moment. Kendrick saw something in Alonso's eyes that he had not seen before. "He's changed," Kendrick thought to himself. "He's not a boy now. He's turned into a man—a man who's made up his mind to fight for his rights."

"Alonso," he said, "I'll keep one eye on the sheep and the other one on you while you practice your shooting. How does that sound to you?"

"That sounds good to me, Bart," Alonso said and drew his gun.

For the next hour, Kendrick watched as Alonso practiced his shooting. Later, they made a fire and cooked themselves something to eat. As he was taking his last piece of food off his plate, Kendrick looked up and stared off into the distance.

"What is it, Bart?" Alonso asked. "Do you see something?"

"No, but I think I hear something." Kendrick put down his plate and got down on both knees. He put his ear to the ground and listened. Then he rose and told Alonso, "there are two riders coming this way—and they are coming fast."

Without another word, Alonso put down his cup of coffee and stood up. He put his hand on his gun and stood shoulder to shoulder with Kendrick. They waited for the two riders to come into the camp.

A minute later Kendrick was not surprised to find that they were again facing McDade and Quinn. Both riders wore evil smiles on their faces.

McDade tapped his tongue against the roof of his mouth. "I see you boys had some trouble last night," he said. "Trouble in the shape of a dead dog and some dead sheep."

"You killed them," Alonso said. "I know you did. Now, if you do not leave here, I will kill you."

"Look at that, McDade," Quinn said, pointing. "The kid has gone and got himself a gun. He's changed since the last time we met up with him. Now, don't that beat all?"

"If you ask me," McDade said, "I don't think he's man enough to use it."

Alonso drew his gun.

McDade drew his gun at the same time. Before Alonso could even take aim, McDade shot the gun out of Alonso's hand. It fell to the ground. As Alonso bent down to pick it up, McDade said, "Don't touch it, kid." Turning to Kendrick, he said, "The kid's trigger-happy. Did you teach him to be that way?"

Kendrick didn't answer. McDade moved his horse close to Alonso, who didn't move an inch. He hit Alonso on the side of the head with his free hand, and said, "Don't you ever throw down on me again, kid. If you do, you're dead. You—"

Suddenly Kendrick reached up, grabbed McDade and pulled him out of the saddle. As he threw him down on the ground, he pulled the gun from McDade's hand and tossed it to Alonso. "Shoot Quinn if he goes for his gun," Kendrick said to him.

"What are you going to do, Bart?" Alonso asked. As he spoke, he kept his eyes and his gun trained on Quinn.

"Teach McDade not to go around killing dogs and poisoning sheep. You did it, didn't you—you and Quinn?"

"You were warned to get out of here," McDade said, looking up at him. "We gave you fair warning. But you didn't listen. So now you've paid the price for staying."

Kendrick bent down and pulled McDade to his feet. Holding the man by his shirt, he drew him close. "I want you and your friend, Quinn, to get out of here right now," Kendrick said coldly. "And from now on, you leave my partner and me alone."

McDade kicked Kendrick, causing Kendrick to lose his hold on him. When he did, McDade hit him in the face. Then he hit him again in the chest, knocking Kendrick to the ground.

Kendrick leaped to his feet and made a grab for McDade. When he had the man in his hands once again, he dragged him to his horse and forced him to climb into the saddle. Then he turned and took McDade's gun from Alonso. He emptied the gun and then gave it back to McDade.

"Now, ride out of here, both of you," Kendrick ordered.

"Kendrick, you sure are one stupid cowboy," McDade said. "Anyone with any sense would have cleared out of here by now."

"You heard me," Kendrick said. "I told you to ride out—now."

"Okay, we'll ride out," McDade said with an evil grin. "But we'll be back. And next time you and that kid had better be gone."

"We've given you two warnings," Quinn added. "Only it looks like you two don't have enough sense to take our warnings to heart. This is the last warning. We want you off this range."

"If I ever see either one of you around here again," Kendrick said, "I'll put a mark or two on you that won't rub off. That's my warning to you."

"You and who else will do that?" McDade, asked, laughing.

"I won't need anyone else to do what needs doing. You very well know that, McDade."

"I never met a horse I couldn't break," McDade shot back. Then he and Quinn turned their horses around and rode off.

"Bart, what should we do now?" Alonso asked as he and Kendrick watched the men ride away.

"We're going to get ready to defend ourselves, to fight. If you feel up to it."

"I do. It will be the two of us against the two of them."

"The first thing we better do is to get the flock to a safe place."

Alonso looked around. "I don't see any place that looks really safe. Maybe we could—" He stopped speaking when he heard Kendrick groan. "What is it, Bart? What's the matter?"

"It looks like McDade and Quinn have run into some of their friends." Kendrick pointed to a hill in the distance where McDade and Quinn had stopped their horses. They were talking to three other men they had just met.

McDade turned in his saddle and pointed toward Kendrick and Alonso.

Then, all five men began to ride toward the camp. Kendrick said, "It looks like we're in for some big trouble this time. Take cover, Alonso."

CHAPTER

9

As Alonso took cover behind a tree, Kendrick said, "We're going to need some help, Alonso. Get your horse and ride to Don Lucero's ranch. Tell him what's happening here. Tell him we need the help of him and his men."

Kendrick drew his gun. Then when Alonso did the same, he barked, "Move, Alonso! Go get help like I told you to."

"It is too late for that now," Alonso told him. "If I left you here alone to face those five men you might be killed. No, I will stay here and we will fight them together."

As the five men rode into camp, McDade shouted, "Drive those sheep that way!"

Three of the men rode toward the flock and when they reached it, they began to drive it to the west.

"We have to stop them, Bart," Alonso said. "There is a cliff in that direction. They are going to drive the sheep over the cliff. They will be killed!"

Before Kendrick could stop him, Alonso jumped to his feet and ran toward his horse. On the way, he stopped to grab the lariat that hung from Kendrick's saddle horn. Leaping into the saddle, he moved his horse straight for the men who were driving the sheep toward the cliff. When he got closer to the men, he swung the lariat in a wide loop above his head.

Alonso threw the lariat. It settled down around the chest of the lead rider. Alonso pulled on the lariat and the man flew off his saddle. The two men behind the fallen man couldn't stop or turn away in time. They ran into the fallen man's horse, which had stopped running when it lost its rider.

Kendrick watched all this from behind a tree. Everything was happening so fast he didn't have any time to act himself. Next, Alonso galloped up to the front of the flock and turned it around. He drove the sheep back toward McDade and Quinn who took aim and fired at him. But Alonso had bent forward and was hugging his horse's neck. Both bullets missed him.

"Stop or I'll shoot!" Kendrick yelled at McDade and Quinn as he stepped out from behind the tree.

They turned, saw Kendrick, and fired at him. Quinn's shot hit Kendrick in the upper part of his left arm. Quinn was about to shoot again when McDade shouted, "Look out, Quinn!"

Suddenly the flock of sheep was running right into them. McDade and Quinn tried hard to get out of the way but it was too late. The running sheep were on all sides of them. Knocked around by the sheep, their horses fell down, throwing McDade and Quinn to the ground.

"I can handle these two," Kendrick shouted to Alonso. "You head back and round up those other three."

Alonso grinned and rode back the way he had come. Kendrick let the flock of sheep go on by him. Then he walked over and aimed his gun at McDade and Quinn, who were back on their feet.

"I wouldn't move if I were you," Kendrick told them. "Who are these three men you brought back here with you, McDade?"

"They work for Mr. Drew, same as Quinn and me. Listen, Kendrick, give us a break, will you? Let us go and we won't give you or the kid any more trouble."

"We were only doing our job," Quinn said, his voice a little more than a whisper.

"That's some bad job you boys have, shooting at people," Kendrick said. He looked in Alonso's direction and was surprised to see that he had captured two of the three men. They were tied back to back. But there was no sign of the third man or of Alonso himself. Kendrick wondered where his partner was—and he began to worry about him.

A few minutes later Alonso came into sight again from around the side of a hill. Marching in front of him at the point of a gun was the third man.

"Move out, you two," Kendrick ordered McDade and Quinn.

"I almost lost one," Alonso said as Kendrick and his prisoners joined him. "One man got away when I was not looking. So I tied up the other two and went for him. I found him hiding behind a tree in the woods."

Someone shouted Alonso's name. Kendrick turned to see Don Lucero and some of his men riding toward them.

"We heard shooting," Don Lucero said when he reached them. "What happened?"

Alonso told him.

"I see you have been shot, Señor Kendrick," Don Lucero said. "You must come back to my ranch. We can take care of your arm there."

"Thank you, Don Lucero," Kendrick said. "I'll be glad to do that. Then Alonso and me can take our prisoners to town and turn them over to the sheriff."

Don Lucero took some money from his pocket. "This is the money I got when I sold the fleece from your sheep, Alonso," he said. "My men and I were just returning from town when we heard the shooting. We came to see what was happening here."

"Thank you, sir," Alonso said as he took the money from Don Lucero. "I plan to use this money to buy some more sheep."

"You and your partner will be able to buy many sheep now," Don Lucero said. "You can buy them with this money and also with the thousand dollars reward money. I want you and your partner to have it—as a gift. By capturing these men you have helped sheep ranchers in this whole territory. You have shown the cattlemen that sheepherders will stand up for their rights. I am proud of you, my young friend."

Alonso was so happy he couldn't speak.

But Kendrick could. "Thank you very much, Don Lucero," he said. "That extra money will be a great help."

Herding the sheep and their prisoners in front of them, Alonso and Kendrick followed Don Lucero and his men back to their ranch. Along the way, Kendrick found himself thinking about Alonso. He thought about how Alonso had captured the three men and turned his flock around. "He did it as well as any cowboy could have done it," Kendrick thought. "Maybe even *better* than some cowboys could have done it."

"I've taught the boy just about everything I know about cowboying," Kendrick thought.

"And it looks like I've turned him into a cowboy, even if he doesn't know it yet." He began to smile.

"Why do you smile, Bart?" Alonso asked.

"Because I just found out that I'm not the last cowboy after all," Kendrick answered.

"What do you mean?" Alonso asked.

"Maybe I'll tell you sometime," Kendrick said as the smile on his face got wider.